YOU CAN MAKE A DIFFERENCE

Why and How Your Christian Life Makes a Difference

EDWARD D. ANDREWS

YOU CAN MAKE A DIFFERENCE

Why and How Your Christian Life Makes a Difference

Edward D. Andrews

Christian Publishing House
Cambridge, Ohio

Copyright © 2017 Edward D. Andrews

All rights reserved. Except for brief quotations in articles, other publications, book reviews, and blogs, no part of this book may be reproduced in any manner without prior written permission from the publishers. For information, write, support@christianpublishers.org

Unless otherwise stated, Scripture quotations are from Updated American Standard Version (UASV) Copyright © 2022 by Christian Publishing House

YOU CAN MAKE A DIFFERENCE: Why and How Your Christian Life Makes a Difference by Edward D. Andrews

ISBN-10: 1945757744

ISBN-13: 978-1945757747

Table of Contents

Book Description 9

Preface 10

Introduction 12

CHAPTER 1 You Can Make a Difference 14

    The Power of One: Understanding the Ripple Effect 14

    Who Are the Difference Makers? 16

CHAPTER 2 The Legacy of Biblical Heroes 19

    David: The Heart of a Servant 19

    Nehemiah: The Power of a Praying Leader 21

    Deborah: A Beacon of Courageous Faith 23

    Esther: The Grace of a Queen and Savior 25

    Apostle Paul: From Persecutor to Proclaimer 27

CHAPTER 3 The Power of Christian Influence 31

    Unpacking the Great Responsibility 31

    Building Bridges through Christ-Like Love 33

    Fostering Community with Compassionate Care 35

CHAPTER 4 Cultivating a Spiritual Attitude 38

    The Heart of Humility 38

    The Power of Patience 40

    The Virtue of Kindness 42

    The Strength of Self-Control 43

CHAPTER 5 Courageous Faith in Action 46

    Unwavering in the Face of Trials 46

    Empowering Others through Faith 48

    Courage, the Catalyst for Change 50

CHAPTER 6 Making a Difference Through Service 53
Serving With a Purpose: The Christian Mission...................... 53
Tangible Love: Caring for the Least of These 55
Mobilizing for Missions: Serving Beyond Borders 57

CHAPTER 7 Living Joyfully in Christ 60
The Joy of the Lord as Our Strength 60
Radiating the Love of Christ.. 62
Fostering a Joyous Christian Community................................ 64

CHAPTER 8 Your Personal Impact 67
The Power of Personal Testimony 67
Empowering Others through Discipleship 69
Making a Difference, One Person at a Time 71

CHAPTER 9 Embracing Your Role as a Difference Maker 74
The Power of Small Gestures 74
Balancing Responsibility with Grace 76
Building a Legacy of Love and Faith.. 78

CHAPTER 10 The Journey of a Difference Maker............80
Celebrating Victories, Big and Small 80
Looking Ahead: Your Ongoing Journey as a Difference Maker 82

APPENDIX A Breaking Free from Negative Patterns: Renewing Your Mind in Christ...84
Recognizing Negative Patterns... 84
Understanding the Power of Renewing Your Mind 87
Challenging Negative Thoughts and Beliefs 90
Embracing the Truth of Your Identity in Christ...................... 93
Practicing Self-Reflection and Prayer...................................... 96

Surrounding Yourself with Positive Influences 99

Walking in Freedom and Transformation 102

APPENDIX B Discovering Your Identity in Christ: Embracing Your True Worth **106**

Understanding Your Identity in Christ 106

Embracing God's Unchanging Word 109

Renewing Your Mind 113

Embracing God's Love and Grace 117

Living Out Your Identity in Christ 120

Overcoming Obstacles and Embracing Victory 124

Walking in God's Purpose for Your Life 128

APPENDIX C Overcoming Self-Doubt with God's Promises: Embracing Your Potential **133**

The Power of God's Promises 133

Identifying and Challenging Self-Doubt 137

Claiming God's Promises of Identity and Worth 143

Renewing Your Mind through Scripture 146

Walking in Faith and Confidence 150

Overcoming Obstacles and Embracing Victory 153

Living Out Your God-Given Potential 157

APPENDIX D Overcoming Comparison and Embracing Your Unique Journey **161**

Recognizing the Trap of Comparison 161

Embracing Your Uniqueness in God's Design 164

Shifting Your Focus to God's Approval 167

Cultivating Gratitude and Contentment 171

Celebrating Others without Comparison 175

Finding Your True Identity in Christ 179

Living Authentically and Pursuing Purpose 183

APPENDIX E Overcoming Self-Criticism: Embracing God's Unconditional Love **188**

Recognizing the Power of Self-Criticism 188

Discovering God's Unconditional Love 192

Challenging Negative Thought Patterns 195

Embracing Forgiveness and Redemption 199

Cultivating Self-Compassion 202

Renewing the Mind with God's Word 206

Walking in Freedom and Confidence 209

BIBLIOGRAPHY **214**

Book Description

In "You Can Make a Difference: Why and How Your Christian Life Makes a Difference," the transformative power of faith is explored through the lens of everyday believers who, like the biblical heroes of yore, have the potential to shape their world through their spirituality and actions. Drawing inspiration from figures like David, Nehemiah, Deborah, Esther, and the Apostle Paul, the book reveals how a Christian life can positively influence others.

This book provides practical insights and inspiration for Christians who strive to live a life of service and make a lasting impact. It underlines the importance of a spiritual attitude, courageous faith, and service to others. By using biblical principles and personal anecdotes, the book elucidates how each believer, no matter how ordinary, has the potential to be an extraordinary force of change.

From fostering community and radiating Christ's love to empowering others through discipleship, "You Can Make a Difference" guides readers on a journey of spiritual growth and service. It serves as a reminder that even small gestures can ripple out to create significant change, and that living out Jesus' teachings is a joyous responsibility.

This book is an uplifting call to action for all Christians to embody their faith, encouraging them to step into their role as difference makers with grace, courage, and joy. Regardless of whether you touch ten lives or just one, this book will inspire you to live out your Christian life with an understanding that you can and will make a difference.

Edward D. Andrews

Preface

As I sit down to write these words, I am acutely aware of the enormity of the task before us as Christians. Jesus' commandment to love one another as He loved us is as profound as it is challenging. In a world that can often feel disconnected, indifferent, and even hostile, how can we as Christians make a difference?

This is the question at the heart of this book. It is a question I have wrestled with, prayed over, and, through God's grace, found insights that I believe can guide us all on our spiritual journeys. The words within these pages are born of that exploration. They echo conversations, prayers, sermons, and, most importantly, God's Word, as we venture together to comprehend our role as Christians in the modern world.

The examples we have from biblical heroes like David, Nehemiah, Deborah, Esther, and Paul show us that each individual, empowered by faith, can indeed make a significant difference. They stood strong in the face of adversity, cared deeply for their people, and displayed a mild, spiritual attitude that guided their actions.

Our calling as Christians is no different. It's not about grand gestures or earth-shattering acts, but everyday choices—moments of kindness, patience, love, and courage. It is in these moments that we touch the lives of others, sometimes in ways we might never fully comprehend.

This book is not intended to be a roadmap, but rather, a compass—providing direction rather than dictating paths. As diverse as we are in our walks of life, so too are our journeys of faith. My hope is that by reading this book, you will find encouragement, inspiration, and perhaps, a new perspective on what it means to be a Christian in today's world.

Remember, no matter where you are in your journey, your Christian life can make a positive difference. You are part of a bigger story, one of faith, hope, and love, and I pray that this book will help you see the integral role you play in that story.

This is a journey we take together, hand in hand, heart to heart. I hope this book encourages and empowers you to realize that yes, you can make a difference. And when you do, it will be a beautiful testament to God's love in action. So, let's embark on this journey together, embracing the joyous responsibility we have been given, with faith as our guide and love as our driving force.

Edward D. Andrews

Author of Over 220 Books

Introduction

In a world filled with nearly eight billion people, the idea of making a significant difference can seem daunting. Our lives are but a drop in this vast ocean of humanity, and it is easy to feel insignificant. Yet, as Christians, we have been called to do just that - make a difference. But what does it mean to make a difference? And how can we, as ordinary individuals, live in a way that our lives resonate beyond our small corners of existence?

Making a difference, at its core, is about effecting change and leaving an impact. It's about touching lives, sparking transformation, and reflecting the love and teachings of Jesus Christ in the world around us. This is the journey we are about to undertake together.

In this book, we will look towards the Bible - our guiding star - to illuminate the way. We will learn from the heroes of our faith, men and women who stood firmly in their convictions, lived out their faith courageously, and thus, shaped the course of history. From David's unwavering belief, to Esther's brave heart, to Paul's radical transformation, their lives exemplify the power of a single person to make a difference.

But this book is not just about the biblical past; it's about the present and our role in it. As followers of Jesus, we are called to be His hands and feet, serving those around us with love and compassion, and ultimately, pointing them towards God. We are called to live out our faith - not just within the confines of a church building, but in our homes, our workplaces, our communities. It is through this everyday living that we reflect Jesus' love to the world.

We will delve into practical ways of making a difference, discovering the transformative power of a spiritual attitude, the courage that springs from unwavering faith, and the joy that comes from service. We will find that making a difference is not a task reserved for a select few, but a calling for every follower of Jesus.

By embracing this calling, we step into a powerful tradition of difference-makers. We become part of a chain reaction of love and faith that can change lives, communities, and ultimately, the world. This is our privilege, and indeed, our responsibility as Christians.

As we embark on this journey together, let us remember this: We are not alone. We have the Bible as our guide, the Holy Spirit as our helper, and a community of believers walking alongside us. Let us step boldly into the calling we have received, confident in the knowledge that through Christ, we can and will make a difference.

CHAPTER 1 You Can Make a Difference

The Power of One: Understanding the Ripple Effect

There's a familiar adage, "Great oaks from little acorns grow." It paints an image of something small and seemingly insignificant giving rise to something mighty and impressive. This metaphor applies beautifully to our Christian journey, emphasizing the potential we each have to effect profound change and make a substantial difference in the world around us.

The Power of One: Understanding the Ripple Effect

Have you ever tossed a stone into a still pond and watched the ripples fan out, reaching far beyond the initial impact point? This is the power of one, the ripple effect that each of us, as Christians, can have in our communities and our world.

In the Bible, we see numerous examples of individuals who, through their faith and obedience to God, created ripple effects that reached far beyond their immediate circumstances. These were ordinary individuals who were used by God to bring about extraordinary change.

Take the story of David, for example. As a shepherd boy, he was the least likely candidate for royalty (1 Samuel 16:11-12). Yet, it was through his humble obedience and unwavering faith in God that he was anointed king and led Israel to many victories, influencing the entire nation and generations to come.

In the New Testament, the Apostle Paul stands out as a beacon of transformative power. Initially, Paul (known then as Saul) was a zealous persecutor of Christians (Acts 9:1, ESV). However, after a divine encounter with Christ, he became one of the most influential apostles, whose letters continue to shape Christian doctrine today.

These biblical examples demonstrate the extraordinary power that a single individual, when aligned with God's will, can have. Each act of faith, each demonstration of obedience, sent ripples of change throughout their communities and even across time.

It is crucial to remember that the power of one is not merely about an individual's strength, wisdom, or abilities. This power finds its foundation in a relationship with God, grounded in a faithful commitment to His Word, the Bible. As stated in John 15:5 (ESV), Jesus said, "I am the vine; you are the branches. Whoever abides in me and I in him, he it is that bears much fruit, for apart from me you can do nothing."

The emphasis here is not on divine intervention, but on a committed Christian life that bears fruit through the active application of biblical principles. Our relationship with God isn't a passive one, nor does it endorse a life of inactivity, waiting for miracles. Instead, it urges us to immerse ourselves in His Word, draw wisdom from it, and then work actively to live out that wisdom in our everyday lives.

It is through this dedicated process of learning, living, and growing in our relationship with God that we cultivate the ability to make a significant difference. As we align our actions with His teachings and strive to live in accordance with His Word, we become equipped and empowered to bear much fruit, not by our might but by living a life true to the teachings of the Bible.

The Power of One in Our Lives

Understanding the power of one – the ripple effect – is not merely a historical or biblical concept; it has practical implications for our lives today.

Each of us has the capacity to influence others positively. Our words, actions, attitudes, and choices can create ripples that touch the lives of those around us. We can make a difference in our families, workplaces, neighborhoods, and beyond by living out the love and teachings of Jesus in our daily interactions. This could be as simple as a kind word to a coworker, helping a neighbor in need, or sharing the hope of the Gospel with someone who is searching.

But, as with the biblical heroes, our ability to create positive ripples hinges on our relationship with God. It is His Spirit moving within us that prompts, guides, and empowers us to live in a way that reflects His love and truth.

The Responsibility and Joy of the Power of One

Recognizing the power of one carries with it a sense of responsibility. We are called to live in a manner worthy of the Gospel (Philippians 1:27, ESV), understanding that our lives are a witness to the world. But this responsibility is not a burdensome obligation; it is a joyous privilege. Through us, God's love reaches out, touches lives, and transforms hearts.

Furthermore, the ripple effect assures us that no act of faith is too small or insignificant. Just as a tiny stone can create expansive ripples, our seemingly small acts of love and obedience can have far-reaching effects. We may not always see the end result of our actions, but we can trust that God uses them for His purposes and glory.

As we embark on this journey of exploring how our Christian lives can make a difference, let us remember the power of one, the ripple effect of our actions. Let us be inspired by the examples of faith in the Bible and encouraged by the potential within each of us. And most importantly, let us rely on God's enabling, knowing that it is through His power at work in us that we can truly make a difference.

Who Are the Difference Makers?

When we reflect upon human history, particular individuals emerge as catalysts of change. These difference makers, through their choices and actions, have significantly influenced their societies and, in many cases, the course of history. Both the Bible and the annals of Christian history provide us with countless examples of such individuals. But what characteristics define these difference makers, and how do they exemplify the principles of difference-making in the context of a Christian life?

Ordinary People, Extraordinary Faith

At first glance, many difference makers may seem like ordinary individuals, but it's their extraordinary faith that sets them apart. They are seldom born into high social status or extraordinary circumstances. Rather, their remarkable journey is rooted in a steadfast adherence to God's Word and an unwavering faith.

Consider Nehemiah, a cupbearer to the king, a role that was in no way indicative of leadership or influence. However, his deep concern for his people and unshakeable faith in God propelled him to become a leader who oversaw the rebuilding of Jerusalem's walls, uniting and strengthening his people in the process (Nehemiah 1-6).

Similarly, in the history of Christianity, we find numerous difference makers who rose from ordinary beginnings to leave indelible marks. John Wycliffe, often called the "Morning Star of the Reformation," was a scholar and theologian. It was his unwavering conviction of the authority of Scripture that led him to translate the Bible into English, making God's Word accessible to common people for the first time in history. His actions laid the groundwork for the Protestant Reformation and changed the course of Christian history.

Courageous and Selfless

A defining characteristic of difference makers is their courage. They demonstrate a willingness to step out of their comfort zones, stand up for their beliefs, and sometimes, risk their own lives for the sake of others.

We see this courage in Deborah, a prophetess of Israel. She stepped into a role of leadership when her nation needed guidance, leading Israel to victory against the oppressive Canaanite king (Judges 4-5). Her bravery and faithfulness continue to inspire us today.

In Christian history, this courage is embodied by figures like Martin Luther, who, driven by a commitment to the truth of the Gospel, sparked the Protestant Reformation. His Ninety-Five Theses challenged the practices of the Church, marking the beginning of a religious revolution. Despite the risks, Luther courageously stood by his convictions, fundamentally transforming Christianity.

Servant-hearted

Difference makers are also marked by their servant hearts. They embody Christ's teaching in Mark 10:45 (ESV), "For even the Son of Man did not come to be served, but to serve, and to give his life as a ransom for many."

In the Bible, the Apostle Paul exemplifies this spirit of service. Once a persecutor of Christians, his transformative encounter with Jesus led him to become a servant of the Gospel, spreading the message of Christ throughout the Roman Empire and writing letters that continue to guide Christians today (Acts 9).

From the annals of Christian history, John Hus, a precursor to the Protestant Reformation, stands out as a servant-hearted difference maker. He championed the cause of church reform and, like Christ, gave his life for the truth of the Gospel.

These profiles offer just a glimpse into the lives of difference makers. Each story underscores the fact that anyone, regardless of their background or circumstances, can make a difference. By fostering a heart for service, displaying courage in the face of adversity, and grounding themselves in an extraordinary faith, difference makers bring about change that can reverberate through generations. The next section will further explore how each of us, as followers of Christ, can cultivate these characteristics and make a positive impact in our world.

CHAPTER 2 The Legacy of Biblical Heroes

David: The Heart of a Servant

David, the shepherd boy who became the king of Israel, is a prominent figure in the Bible whose life offers profound insights into the heart of a servant. The narrative of David's life, with its trials, triumphs, failures, and faith, illustrates that being a servant isn't just about our actions, but is deeply connected to our attitude, outlook, and our relationship with God.

David: A Humble Beginning

David's journey begins in the humblest of circumstances, tending his father's sheep in the fields. When Samuel the prophet was seeking a king to anoint, David was the least expected candidate, the youngest son of Jesse, out in the fields while his elder brothers were presented to Samuel (1 Samuel 16:11, ASV). But God sees beyond appearances, looking at the heart (1 Samuel 16:7, ASV). David was chosen not for his physical strength or stature, but because of his heart, a heart aligned with God's own.

A Heart After God's Own

David's relationship with God is one of the most striking aspects of his life. He had a heart "after God's own heart" (1 Samuel 13:14, ASV). This was reflected in his deep trust in God, seen when he faced Goliath, the Philistine giant. David, a young shepherd, armed with only a sling and a few stones, was not intimidated by Goliath's size or his intimidating armor. His faith in God was unwavering, and he believed that God, who delivered him from the lion and the bear, would deliver him from this Philistine (1 Samuel 17:37, ASV).

A Servant's Response to Trials

The trials and tribulations that David faced, particularly the persecution by King Saul, further reveal his servant's heart. Despite being anointed to be king, David spent years in hiding, fleeing from Saul who sought to kill him. Yet, when given the opportunity, David refused to harm Saul, the Lord's anointed king (1 Samuel 24:6, ASV). David's response to Saul's relentless pursuit reveals a heart that respected God's authority and timing.

Repentance and Restoration

David, despite being a man after God's own heart, was not without flaws. He committed grave sins, including adultery and murder. However, when confronted with his sins by the prophet Nathan, David genuinely repented (2 Samuel 12:13, ASV). His heartfelt cry for forgiveness is documented in Psalm 51, where he pleaded with God for mercy and cleansing. This repentance was not just about seeking forgiveness, but about restoring his relationship with God, a crucial aspect of a servant's heart.

Legacy of a Servant

David's legacy is that of a man whose heart was attuned to God, a man who served God's purposes in his generation (Acts 13:36, ESV). His life teaches us that a servant is someone who trusts God wholeheartedly, respects God's authority, waits patiently for His timing, and when they falter and fail, they return to God in genuine repentance.

David's life underscores the truth that making a difference does not require us to be perfect, but to have a heart that seeks after God. As we strive to serve and make a difference in our world, may our prayer echo David's own words, "Create in me a clean heart, O God; and renew a right spirit within me" (Psalm 51:10, ASV). The life of David, the servant-hearted king, serves as an inspiring testament of how an ordinary individual can make extraordinary differences when their heart is aligned with God's. Let's explore how we can nurture such a heart in the next chapter.

Nehemiah was a Jewish leader who oversaw the rebuilding of Jerusalem in the mid-5th century BCE after its destruction by the Babylonians. He was a cupbearer for the king of Persia and lived far away from his home, but he remained faithful and persevered in the face of difficulty. In addition to his work in rebuilding Jerusalem, Nehemiah is also known for his fervent and continual prayers.

Nehemiah: The Power of a Praying Leader

Among the Biblical heroes who made a remarkable difference, Nehemiah stands out as a leader who changed the course of a nation through the power of prayer and decisive action. Serving as the cupbearer to the Persian king Artaxerxes in the 5th century B.C.E., Nehemiah's story unfolds to reveal a man whose leadership was firmly rooted in his profound relationship with God.

Nehemiah: A Man of Prayer

The book of Nehemiah opens with Nehemiah hearing about the desperate state of Jerusalem, its walls broken down and its gates burned (Nehemiah 1:3, ASV). His response to this distressing news reveals the first noteworthy aspect of his character: Nehemiah was a man of prayer. Upon hearing the news, he "sat down and wept and mourned for days, and he continued fasting and praying before the God of heaven" (Nehemiah 1:4, ESV).

In his prayer, Nehemiah not only laments the broken state of Jerusalem but also confesses the sins of his people and his family, acknowledging their rebellion against God (Nehemiah 1:6, ASV). His prayer is heartfelt and sincere, underlining the depth of his relationship with God and his understanding of the spiritual root of Israel's predicament.

Prayer Leading to Action

Nehemiah's prayers were not mere rituals or expressions of despair. They were instead the prelude to decisive action. When King Artaxerxes noticed Nehemiah's sadness and asked him why he was sad, Nehemiah was afraid, but he prayed to God and answered the king honestly (Nehemiah 2:2-5, ASV). His prayers led him to articulate his desire to go to Jerusalem and rebuild its walls. Nehemiah's prayers were his divine connection, guiding him in his leadership role.

Leadership Through Opposition

Nehemiah's leadership was constantly tested through opposition from various quarters. Yet, in every challenge he faced, Nehemiah's response was to turn to God in prayer. When Sanballat and Tobiah mocked the Jews and attempted to demoralize them, Nehemiah's response was prayer and further dedication to the task at hand (Nehemiah 4:4-6, ASV). His praying leadership was not about passive acceptance but active engagement with the situation, guided by his unwavering faith in God.

Nehemiah: A Legacy of Praying Leadership

The legacy Nehemiah left was that of a leader whose reliance on God, expressed through continual prayer, led to the physical and spiritual rebuilding of a nation. The walls of Jerusalem were rebuilt in a mere 52 days (Nehemiah 6:15, ASV), a miraculous accomplishment by any standard. But more than the physical restoration, Nehemiah's leadership marked a spiritual revival among the people, as they rediscovered the law and renewed their covenant with God (Nehemiah 8, ASV).

Nehemiah's story teaches us that making a difference in our world requires leaders willing to pray and act. As we commit ourselves to God in prayer, and allow that prayer to guide our actions, we align ourselves with His purposes and power. Like Nehemiah, we can then become catalysts for change and restoration, making a significant difference in the places and lives God calls us to. As we engage with our world, may we too cultivate a spirit of praying leadership, continually seeking God's guidance and strength for the tasks at hand.

Deborah: A Beacon of Courageous Faith

In the annals of biblical heroes, few shine as brightly as Deborah, a prophetess, judge, and a motivator of a military leader, Barak. Her story, recorded in Judges 4-5, resonates powerfully in our hearts, reminding us of the courage and faith necessary to make a difference.

Deborah: A Prophetess and Judge

The book of Judges introduces Deborah as a prophetess who was judging Israel at that time (Judges 4:4, ASV). She sat under the palm tree of Deborah between Ramah and Bethel in the hill country of Ephraim, and the Israelites came up to her for judgment. Her leadership role in a predominantly male society was remarkable for her time, and it speaks volumes about her wisdom, character, and God's favor.

An Instrument of God's Will

Deborah was not only a judge but also a prophetess, someone who delivered messages from God. When the Israelites were being harshly oppressed by Jabin, the king of Canaan, Deborah sent for Barak and relayed God's commands: "Hasn't the Lord, the God of Israel, commanded you: 'Go, muster the troops from Naphtali and Zebulun at Mount Tabor, taking 10,000 men with you?'" (Judges 4:6, ASV). As a leader, she didn't let her personal feelings or societal norms dictate her actions; she courageously delivered God's message, promoting God's will over man's.

Courageous Faith in Action

When Barak was hesitant to go into battle without Deborah, she agreed to accompany him, but prophesied that the honor of killing Sisera, the Canaanite commander, would go to a woman (Judges 4:9, ASV). Deborah's courage was rooted in her faith in God. She was willing to step into a war zone because she trusted God's promises.

Deborah: Leading a Nation to Victory

The courage of Deborah is also seen in her leading a nation to victory through her guidance of Barak. She, along with Barak, led the Israelites into battle against Sisera and the Canaanites. Deborah's faith became a beacon for the entire nation, leading them to a significant victory, as "all the army of Sisera fell by the edge of the sword; not a man was left" (Judges 4:16, ASV).

A Legacy of Courageous Faith

After their victory, Deborah and Barak sang a song, found in Judges 5, praising God for the deliverance He brought about. The song of Deborah serves as a testament to her faith and courageous leadership, reminding future generations of God's faithfulness to those who trust in Him.

Deborah's life offers a potent reminder that courageous faith is not the absence of fear or uncertainty. It is the willingness to move forward in God's direction, regardless of the circumstances or odds. Like Deborah, we are called to be beacons of courageous faith in our spheres of influence, allowing God to work through us to make a difference.

As we seek to make a difference in our world, may we, like Deborah, respond to God's call with courageous faith. May we trust in His promises and allow Him to work through us, even when circumstances seem daunting. For with God, no challenge is too great, and no individual is too small to make a difference.

Esther: The Grace of a Queen and Savior

Esther, a young Jewish woman who became Queen of Persia, stands tall in the annals of biblical history, exemplifying grace under pressure and courage in the face of danger. Her story, narrated in the Book of Esther, provides an extraordinary account of how an individual can make a remarkable difference when guided by faith and courage.

Esther: An Unexpected Queen

Raised by her cousin Mordecai after the death of her parents, Esther's life took an unexpected turn when King Ahasuerus ordered a search for a new queen. Esther, known for her beauty and grace, was chosen above all the other young women in the kingdom (Esther 2:7,

17, ASV). Yet, it was not her physical beauty alone that defined her; Esther was also wise, strategic, and above all, faithful.

A Graceful Savior

Esther's greatest challenge came when Haman, the king's advisor, plotted to destroy the Jews residing in Persia (Esther 3:8-9, ASV). Upon learning of this plan, Mordecai urged Esther to approach the king, an act punishable by death if done without an invitation (Esther 4:11, ASV). Undeterred, Esther requested the Jews to fast for three days, doing so herself as well, and then courageously went before the king (Esther 4:16, ASV).

Boldly Facing the King

When Esther approached Ahasuerus unbidden—a punishable offense, he extended his scepter, signifying that her life was spared. She then invited him and Haman to a banquet. It was here, after a second banquet, that Esther bravely revealed her Jewish identity and Haman's plot to annihilate her people (Esther 7:3-6, ASV). Her bold action led to the hanging of Haman and the issuance of a new decree allowing the Jews to defend themselves against their enemies (Esther 7:10; 8:11, ASV).

A Queen's Legacy

Esther's legacy lies in her courage to step beyond the confines of her safety for the sake of her people. Despite the risk, she chose to act, driven by her love for her people and her faith in God. By her actions, she saved her people from certain death, exemplifying what it means to be a difference-maker.

Making a Difference Like Esther

Esther's life serves as a potent reminder of how faith, courage, and grace can enable us to make a difference. She did not allow the potential risks to deter her from standing up for her people. Even when faced with the threat of death, she placed her trust in God and stood resolute in her faith.

We too can make a difference in our spheres of influence, like Esther, by embracing courage, standing up for what is right, and trusting in God's sovereignty and timing. The life of Esther is a testament to the significant impact one person can make when guided by faith and courage, proving that in God's hands, ordinary people can do extraordinary things.

As we seek to make a difference in our world, may we, like Esther, stand with grace and courage, placing our faith in God. For when God is with us, no obstacle is insurmountable, and no individual is too small to make a difference.

Apostle Paul: From Persecutor to Proclaimer

The Apostle Paul, formerly known as Saul, has a unique and extraordinary story that embodies the transformative power of faith and God's grace. A fervent persecutor of Christians, Paul experienced a radical conversion that transformed him into one of the greatest proclaimers of the Gospel.

Paul: The Persecutor

Before his conversion, Paul, then known as Saul, was a devout Pharisee committed to preserving the Jewish law and tradition. Saul saw the emerging Christian movement as a threat to Judaism and zealously persecuted Christians. He was present at Stephen's execution (Acts 7:58, ESV), and later, he launched a fierce campaign against the Christians in Jerusalem, imprisoning both men and women (Acts 8:3, ESV).

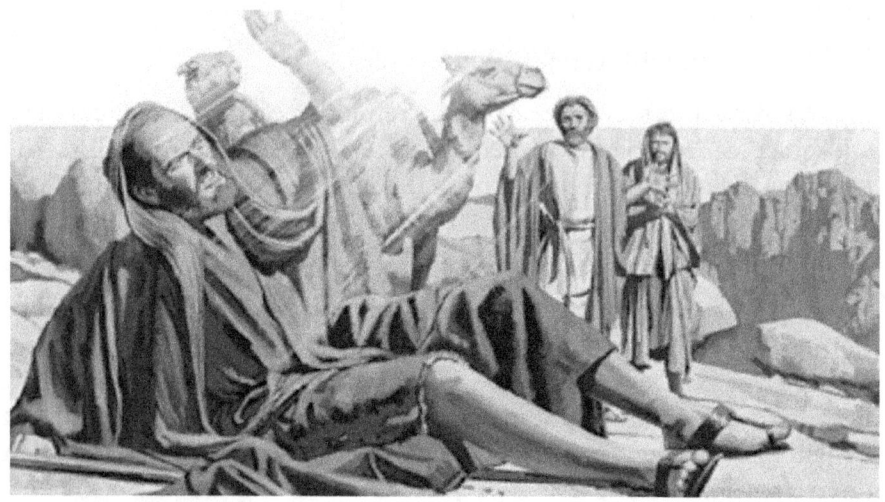

A Radical Conversion

Saul's life took a dramatic turn on the road to Damascus. A blinding light from heaven struck him, and he heard the voice of Jesus asking, "Saul, Saul, why are you persecuting me?" (Acts 9:4, ESV). This encounter marked the beginning of Saul's transformation. He was blinded for three days and did not eat or drink anything. Ananias, a disciple of Jesus in Damascus, was instructed in a vision to go and lay his hands on Saul to restore his sight (Acts 9:10-12, ESV). This event wasn't just about restoring physical sight, but also marked the opening of Saul's spiritual eyes to the truth of the Gospel.

Paul: The Proclaimer

Following his conversion, Saul took the name Paul, signifying his new identity in Christ. Filled with the Holy Spirit, Paul began preaching the Gospel, emphasizing the death and resurrection of Jesus Christ. His teachings were met with skepticism, especially considering his reputation as a former persecutor (Acts 9:21, ESV). Yet, Paul did not allow doubt to deter his mission.

Paul's Missionary Journeys

Over the next three decades, Paul embarked on several missionary journeys across the Roman Empire. He visited regions such as Galatia, Ephesus, Macedonia, and Corinth, among others, spreading the Gospel and establishing Christian communities. His tireless efforts earned him the title of the "Apostle to the Gentiles."

The Legacy of Paul

Paul's ministry has left an indelible mark on Christian history. His letters, known as the Pauline Epistles, form a significant portion of the New Testament and continue to be foundational texts for Christian theology and ethics. His teachings have shaped Christian understanding of key concepts such as grace, faith, the law, and the nature of Christ.

Paul's life story is a testament to the transformative power of God's grace. His conversion demonstrates that no one is beyond the reach of God's love and mercy.

Making a Difference Like Paul

Like Paul, we too can experience transformative grace that enables us to make a difference. Despite his past as a persecutor, Paul allowed God's grace to change him, and he used his past to illustrate the power of Christ's redemption. He took the Gospel to different parts of the world, faced numerous trials and hardships, and remained faithful until the end.

Paul's life is an encouraging reminder that our past does not define us. God's grace is sufficient to transform our lives, and His power is made perfect in our weaknesses (2 Corinthians 12:9, ESV). It is never too late for anyone to make a difference.

May Paul's story inspire us to embrace God's grace, let it transform us, and motivate us to make a difference in our world. As we seek to follow Christ, let us remember Paul's words, "I can do all things through him who strengthens me" (Philippians 4:13, ESV). Paul's life is a shining example that when we allow God to work in and through us, we can indeed make a difference.

CHAPTER 3 The Power of Christian Influence

Unpacking the Great Responsibility

The lives of believers hold a powerful potential to impact others. This chapter delves into the profound implications of Christian influence, highlighting the immense responsibility believers bear in representing Christ to the world.

The Power of Christian Influence

Christian influence is the capacity to affect others positively through our Christian lifestyle. It's about reflecting the values and teachings of Christ in our actions, words, and decisions. Christian influence, however, is not about coercion or imposition; it's about inspiring change through the demonstration of Christ-like love, mercy, and righteousness.

In the Sermon on the Mount, Jesus refers to His followers as the "salt of the earth" and "light of the world" (Matthew 5:13-14, ESV). These metaphors encapsulate the essence of Christian influence. Salt, in the context of the first century, was valuable for its preserving and flavoring properties. Similarly, Christians are called to preserve the faith and add flavor to the world through godly living. As light, we are to illuminate the world with truth, driving out darkness and guiding others towards God.

The Responsibility of Christian Influence

Christian influence carries with it a significant responsibility. As believers, our lives are a testament to our faith and can draw people towards or push them away from God. Our influence should, therefore, always align with the principles and teachings of the Bible.

Paul encourages believers in Ephesus to "walk in a manner worthy of the calling to which you have been called" (Ephesians 4:1, ESV). He reminds us that our actions and words should mirror the character of Christ, in humility, gentleness, and patience, showing forbearance and love to one another. This responsibility is not to be taken lightly. We are, after all, ambassadors for Christ (2 Corinthians 5:20, ESV), representing Him in the world.

Unpacking the Responsibility

Unpacking the responsibility of Christian influence involves understanding that our actions and words matter, and each choice we make can either honor or dishonor God.

Firstly, it implies living out our faith in everyday life. The mundane activities of life may seem insignificant, but they are opportunities to display the love of Christ.

Secondly, it involves setting a Christ-like example. As Paul instructed Timothy, "set the believers an example in speech, in conduct, in love, in faith, in purity" (1 Timothy 4:12, ESV).

Thirdly, we are called to share the Gospel message with others. This does not always mean preaching on a street corner. Often, it is through our actions and love towards others that the Gospel is most effectively shared.

Lastly, it involves standing firm in our faith, even in the face of opposition or persecution. This is not easy, but it is vital for maintaining the integrity of our witness.

Making a Difference Through Influence

Understanding and embracing the power of Christian influence can significantly impact our world. We have been given a great responsibility as believers to make a difference in the world around us. This should not be seen as a burden but rather a privilege.

We have the opportunity to spread love, justice, mercy, and truth in a world that desperately needs it. Our influence, however, can only be as impactful as our willingness to live in obedience to God and His word.

As we continue our Christian journey, let us remember the words of the Apostle Paul, "Therefore, my beloved brothers, be steadfast, immovable, always abounding in the work of the Lord, knowing that in the Lord your labor is not in vain" (1 Corinthians 15:58, ESV). May these words inspire us to use our influence wisely, striving to make a difference in the world for the glory of God.

Building Bridges through Christ-Like Love

In our pursuit of making a difference, one of the most effective tools we wield is love. Genuine, selfless, Christ-like love has the power to build bridges, foster understanding, and inspire transformative change. This section delves into the dynamics of love as a potent form of Christian influence.

Understanding Christ-Like Love

In the New Testament, we encounter a Greek word for love that encapsulates the essence of Christian love—agape. This form of love is selfless, sacrificial, and unconditional, reflecting the very nature of God's love for humanity (Romans 5:8, ESV). It is the love that compelled Jesus to lay down His life for us (John 15:13, ESV). As Christians, we are called to exhibit this kind of love towards others.

When asked about the greatest commandment, Jesus replied, "You shall love the Lord your God with all your heart and with all your soul and with all your mind...and...You shall love your neighbor as yourself" (Matthew 22:37-39, ESV). Our faith, therefore, places love at its core, be it our love for God or our love for people.

Building Bridges through Love

One of the most remarkable aspects of love is its ability to bridge gaps—be it differences in beliefs, cultures, or experiences. Love enables us to connect with others on a fundamental human level, reflecting our shared image-bearing nature (Genesis 1:27, ASV).

Building bridges through love involves several key elements:

Empathy: Christ-like love involves putting ourselves in the shoes of others, understanding their feelings, perspectives, and struggles

(Romans 12:15, ESV). It's about recognizing shared humanity and validating others' experiences.

Respect: Love respects the dignity and worth of every individual, appreciating their unique God-given identity and potential (James 3:9, ESV). It's about seeing beyond superficial differences to the image of God in every person.

Humility: Love is not arrogant or condescending; instead, it embraces humility (1 Corinthians 13:4, ESV). It's about putting others' needs and interests above our own (Philippians 2:3-4, ESV).

Kindness and Generosity: Love motivates us to show kindness and extend generosity towards others (Ephesians 4:32, ESV). Whether through acts of service or the sharing of resources, love compels us to contribute positively to the lives of others.

Sharing the Gospel in Love

While it's essential to share the truth of the Gospel, it's equally important to do so in love (Ephesians 4:15, ESV). In evangelism, love builds trust and creates an open and receptive atmosphere for the message of Christ. It's about reflecting God's love so vividly that people can't help but be drawn to Him.

Conclusion: The Transformative Power of Love

Love has an extraordinary power to influence and inspire change. As we live out Christ's love, we serve as His ambassadors, influencing our world one life at a time. This love, the agape love, bridges gaps, fosters understanding, and transforms hearts. It is the love that can make a profound difference.

Indeed, as the Apostle Paul wrote, "And above all these put on love, which binds everything together in perfect harmony" (Colossians 3:14, ESV). May we, as followers of Christ, put on love every day, influencing the world around us and truly making a difference.

Fostering Community with Compassionate Care

The Christian call is more than an individual journey. It is a communal experience, rooted in the bonds of fellowship, mutual care, and shared purpose. One of the ways we can powerfully influence as Christians is by nurturing a compassionate community. This segment will explore how compassionate care fosters a community that not only reflects Christ's love but also stands as a testament to His transformative power.

Compassionate Care in the Christian Context

Compassion is at the heart of Jesus' ministry. It was compassion that moved Him to heal the sick, feed the hungry, and ultimately give His life for our redemption (Mark 1:41; Matthew 15:32; John 3:16, ESV). Compassionate care, in the Christian context, is an active, tangible expression of love—it is about sharing in the sufferings of others and endeavoring to alleviate their burdens.

The Apostle Paul exhorts us to "Rejoice with those who rejoice, weep with those who weep" (Romans 12:15, ESV). It's a call to engage empathetically with our community, participating in their joys and sorrows. Compassionate care goes beyond mere sentiment; it involves practical actions to meet physical, emotional, and spiritual needs.

Fostering Community through Compassionate Care

Compassionate care plays a vital role in building strong, resilient Christian communities. It serves as the practical outworking of our faith, and it brings to life the teachings of Jesus in a compelling and relatable way.

Here are some key ways compassionate care helps foster community:

Cultivating Unity: Acts of compassionate care foster a sense of unity and shared purpose. As we support one another in times of need, we embody the truth of 1 Corinthians 12:26 (ESV), which says, "If one member suffers, all suffer together; if one member is honored, all rejoice together."

Demonstrating God's Love: Our compassionate actions provide a tangible demonstration of God's love. As Jesus said, "By this everyone will know that you are my disciples, if you love one another" (John 13:35, ESV). Compassionate care is an influential witness to both believers and non-believers.

Empowering Individuals: When we show compassionate care, we not only meet immediate needs but also empower individuals for the long term. Our actions can inspire hope, build confidence, and encourage personal growth, leading to stronger, healthier communities.

Promoting Peace and Reconciliation: Compassionate care aids in the process of peace-building and reconciliation. By caring for those in conflict or pain, we reflect the peace and reconciliation offered by Christ (Ephesians 2:14-16, ESV), promoting healing within our communities.

Responding to Needs in Love

In the parable of the Good Samaritan, Jesus presents a powerful model of compassionate care (Luke 10:25-37, ESV). The Samaritan saw a need, had compassion, and responded with practical care, providing for the injured man's needs without expecting anything in return. This is the model we, as Christians, should strive to emulate in our communities.

Conclusion: The Impact of Compassionate Care

Fostering community with compassionate care has profound implications. As we respond to the needs of those around us with Christ-like compassion, we build robust, resilient communities that reflect the Kingdom of God on earth. And in doing so, we extend the reach of our Christian influence, making a tangible difference in our world.

In the words of the Apostle Paul, "Therefore, as we have opportunity, let us do good to all people, especially to those who belong to the family of believers" (Galatians 6:10, ESV). May we seize every opportunity to demonstrate compassionate care, fostering community and embodying the transformative love of Christ.

CHAPTER 4 Cultivating a Spiritual Attitude

The Heart of Humility

Humility is at the core of a believer's spiritual attitude. Jesus Himself modeled it, teaching and living out the importance of a humble heart. This chapter will delve into the biblical concept of humility, why it matters, and how to cultivate it in our lives.

Understanding Biblical Humility

Humility, as depicted in the Bible, is the recognition of our rightful place before God and others. It is about acknowledging our limitations, surrendering self-interests, and valuing others above ourselves. In the words of the Apostle Paul, "Do nothing from selfish ambition or conceit, but in humility count others more significant than yourselves" (Philippians 2:3, ESV).

Jesus Christ is our ultimate example of humility. Though He was God, He took on the form of a servant and humbled Himself to the point of death, even death on a cross (Philippians 2:5-8, ESV). The depth of His humility is a model for us to follow.

The Importance of Humility

Humility is a prerequisite for a healthy spiritual life and significant Christian influence. Its importance is highlighted in multiple ways throughout Scripture:

Humility Attracts God's Grace: The Scripture says, "God opposes the proud but gives grace to the humble" (James 4:6, ESV). A humble heart is a vessel ready to receive God's grace.

Humility Leads to Wisdom: Proverbs 11:2 (ESV) states, "When pride comes, then comes disgrace, but with the humble is wisdom." Humility allows us to be teachable and open to divine wisdom.

Humility Promotes Unity: Humility helps foster unity among believers. When we humbly regard others as better than ourselves, we create a spirit of mutual respect and harmony (Ephesians 4:2, ESV).

Cultivating Humility in Our Lives

While humility is vital to our spiritual growth, it doesn't come naturally to our fallen nature. It's something we must consciously cultivate in our hearts and minds. Here are some practical ways to foster humility:

Reflect on the Life of Christ: The life of Jesus provides a living blueprint for humility. Studying His words, actions, and attitudes will help us understand and emulate His humility (Matthew 11:29, ESV).

Acknowledge Our Dependence on God: Recognizing our complete dependence on God helps foster humility. As we acknowledge our limitations and rely on His strength, we become more humble (2 Corinthians 3:5, ESV).

Serve Others: Serving others allows us to express humility in practical ways. Jesus demonstrated this when He washed His disciples' feet, teaching them that no task is beneath us when done in love (John 13:1-17, ESV).

Practice Self-Reflection: Regular self-reflection can promote humility. As we honestly evaluate our attitudes and actions in the light of Scripture, we gain a more accurate perspective of ourselves (Lamentations 3:40, ESV).

Conclusion: The Impact of Humility

Humility, a mark of Christlikeness, has profound implications for our spiritual lives and Christian influence. A humble heart receives grace, gains wisdom, fosters unity, and positions us to be used by God in significant ways.

As Proverbs 22:4 (ESV) states, "The reward for humility and fear of the LORD is riches and honor and life." May we, as followers of Christ, continually strive to cultivate a spirit of humility, knowing it aligns us with God's heart and positions us for His purposes.

The Power of Patience

As Christians, the cultivation of spiritual attitudes is paramount in our journey of faith. Among these, patience is a virtue frequently extolled in the scriptures. Patience, in its essence, is an enduring perseverance through challenges, waiting upon the Lord's timing. It's a virtue that defines Christian character and influences our interactions with others. This chapter delves into understanding biblical patience, its importance, and how to cultivate it in our Christian life.

Understanding Biblical Patience

In the Bible, patience is not mere passive waiting; it's active endurance, steadfastness, and perseverance. Consider James' admonition, "Count it all joy, my brothers, when you meet trials of various kinds, for you know that the testing of your faith produces steadfastness" (James 1:2-3, ESV). Here, steadfastness, often translated as patience, emerges not from passivity but from enduring challenges.

Moreover, patience isn't just about circumstances but also about people. Paul instructs us in Ephesians 4:2 (ESV), "with all humility and gentleness, with patience, bearing with one another in love." Patience enables us to show love and grace towards others, even when they are challenging.

The Importance of Patience

Patience is more than a moral virtue—it's an integral component of a healthy Christian life. It's importance can be seen in several key areas:

Patience as a Fruit of the Spirit: As listed in Galatians 5:22-23 (ESV), patience is part of the fruit of the Spirit—a visible manifestation of the Spirit's work in a believer's life.

Patience in Endurance: Patience equips us to endure difficulties faithfully. As James reminds us, "the steadfastness of Job" (James 5:11, ESV) exemplifies patient endurance amid suffering.

Patience in Evangelism: Patience is essential in evangelism and discipleship. We need to patiently sow the seeds of the Gospel, nurture new believers, and trust in God's timing for growth (2 Timothy 2:24-25, ESV).

Cultivating Patience in Our Lives

Patience isn't natural to our impatient human nature—it's a virtue that we must deliberately cultivate. Here's how we can foster patience:

Lean on the Holy Spirit: Since patience is a fruit of the Spirit, we can ask the Holy Spirit to develop this virtue in us. Regular prayer and submission to God's Spirit can grow patience in our lives (Galatians 5:25, ESV).

Study Biblical Examples: Studying biblical characters who exhibited patience can provide us with practical examples to emulate. Characters like Job, Joseph, and the Apostle Paul demonstrate patience in various circumstances.

Practice Patience: Daily life offers numerous opportunities to practice patience—in traffic, in line at the grocery store, with difficult people. Embrace these moments as opportunities to grow in patience.

Rest in God's Sovereignty: Trusting in God's timing and control over our circumstances can help us be patient. As Psalm 37:7 (ESV) says, "Be still before the Lord and wait patiently for him."

Conclusion: The Impact of Patience

Patience is a powerful virtue that profoundly influences our spiritual growth and relationships. As we cultivate patience, we reflect God's character, enhance our witness, and become more resilient in our faith.

As we grow in patience, we come to echo the words of the Psalmist: "I waited patiently for the Lord; he inclined to me and heard my cry" (Psalm 40:1, ESV). This patient waiting is not in vain, but a transformative process that shapes us more into the likeness of Christ, enabling us to make a significant Christian difference.

The Virtue of Kindness

The Christian life is characterized by a myriad of spiritual attitudes, but one of the most powerful and transformative is kindness. Rooted deeply in the nature of God Himself, kindness is a virtue that permeates the Bible, punctuating stories, teachings, and the very character of Christ. This chapter seeks to unpack the importance of kindness, understanding it from a biblical perspective, and practical ways to cultivate it in our daily lives.

Understanding Biblical Kindness

Biblical kindness, or "chesed" in the Hebrew and "chrēstotēs" in the Greek, is not merely an act but an attitude of the heart that is reflected in actions. It signifies a spirit of love and compassion towards others, often resulting in generous and beneficial actions.

As believers, our supreme example of kindness is Jesus Christ. In his earthly ministry, Jesus extended kindness to all people regardless of their social status, ethnicity, or past. His healing of the lepers (Mark 1:40-45, ESV), His encounter with the Samaritan woman at the well (John 4:7-30, ESV), and His forgiveness of the woman caught in adultery (John 8:1-11, ESV) all demonstrate the profound kindness of Christ.

The Importance of Kindness

The value of kindness in a believer's life cannot be overstated. Here's why:

Kindness Reflects God's Character: The Bible repeatedly describes God as kind. His loving-kindness is praised throughout the scriptures (Psalm 136, ESV). As we show kindness, we reflect God's character to others.

Kindness Is a Fruit of the Spirit: Kindness is a part of the fruit of the Spirit listed in Galatians 5:22 (ESV). It's an evidence of the Holy Spirit's work within us.

Kindness Influences Others: Kindness has the power to soften hearts and open doors for the gospel. Romans 2:4 (ESV) teaches that God's kindness leads us to repentance.

Cultivating Kindness in Our Lives

Cultivating kindness requires intentionality, effort, and reliance on the Holy Spirit. Here are some practical steps to grow in kindness:

Reflect on God's Kindness: Regularly pondering God's kindness towards us in Christ can inspire us to extend kindness to others (Ephesians 2:7, ESV).

Pray for Kindness: We can ask God to fill us with His Spirit and produce the fruit of kindness in our lives (Galatians 5:22, ESV).

Practice Kindness: Look for daily opportunities to show kindness to others. This could be in words, actions, or attitudes.

Study Examples of Kindness in the Bible: Stories like the Good Samaritan (Luke 10:25-37, ESV) and Ruth's loyalty to Naomi (Ruth 1:16-17, ESV) provide practical examples of kindness.

Conclusion: The Impact of Kindness

Kindness has a profound impact, both on the individual exercising it and those who receive it. As we grow in kindness, we not only become more like Christ, but we also make a tangible difference in the lives of those around us.

Let us be encouraged by the words of the Apostle Paul: "Therefore, as God's chosen people, holy and dearly loved, clothe yourselves with compassion, kindness, humility, gentleness and patience" (Colossians 3:12, ESV). This call to kindness is an invitation to participate in God's work of transformation in us and through us. Through the virtue of kindness, we truly can make a difference.

The Strength of Self-Control

In the grand tapestry of Christian life, one strand that stands out for its crucial importance is self-control. Often seen as a marker of personal strength, self-control has profound spiritual implications and is a virtue highly esteemed in the Scriptures. This chapter will delve into understanding self-control from a biblical perspective and how we can cultivate it in our spiritual journey.

Understanding Biblical Self-Control

In the Greek New Testament, the word for self-control is "egkrateia," meaning "mastery, holding in, the ability to take hold of oneself." Self-control isn't merely about willpower; it is about controlling one's thoughts, actions, and feelings, aligning them with God's will.

The Apostle Paul particularly highlights self-control in his writings. For instance, in Galatians 5:23 (ESV), he lists it as part of the fruit of the Spirit, integral to a life led by the Holy Spirit. In 1 Corinthians 9:25 (ESV), he employs the metaphor of an athlete exercising self-control in all things to illustrate the discipline required in the Christian life.

The Importance of Self-Control

Self-control serves as an essential framework for the believer's life. Here's why:

Self-Control Reflects God's Nature: Just as with kindness, self-control is an aspect of the divine nature that we should emulate. God exercises control over His creation and His actions.

Self-Control Is a Fruit of the Spirit: As previously mentioned, self-control is part of the Spirit's fruit, indicating a life guided and empowered by the Holy Spirit (Galatians 5:22-23, ESV).

Self-Control Is Crucial for Effective Christian Living: The New Testament underscores the importance of self-control for living a life that pleases God and serves others effectively (1 Peter 1:5-7, ESV).

Cultivating Self-Control in Our Lives

Developing self-control is not merely a matter of personal effort. It involves relying on the Holy Spirit and taking practical steps:

Recognize the Holy Spirit's Role: Self-control is ultimately a gift from God, produced in us by the Holy Spirit. We need to lean on the Spirit in our struggle against sin and for godliness.

Identify Areas for Growth: Each of us has areas where we particularly struggle to exercise self-control. Identifying these areas is an important first step towards growth.

Take Small Steps: Self-control is often developed in small steps. Starting with smaller challenges can build our self-control 'muscles,' preparing us for larger ones.

Stay Accountable: Accountability to fellow believers can be highly beneficial. Sharing our struggles and victories can provide encouragement and motivation.

Conclusion: The Impact of Self-Control

Self-control can significantly shape our Christian witness and effectiveness. A believer who exhibits self-control demonstrates the transformative power of the gospel and the indwelling Spirit.

Remember the words of Peter, "For this very reason, make every effort to supplement your faith with virtue, and virtue with knowledge, and knowledge with self-control, and self-control with steadfastness, and steadfastness with godliness" (2 Peter 1:5-6, ESV).

Self-control, thus, isn't just about personal mastery or achievement; it's about becoming more Christ-like and letting His power shine through us. This is how we truly make a difference.

Edward D. Andrews

CHAPTER 5 Courageous Faith in Action

Unwavering in the Face of Trials

The Christian faith is more than a set of beliefs; it is a way of life marked by trust in God and endurance in the face of trials. This chapter focuses on how we can be unwavering in our faith when confronted with life's challenges.

Understanding Biblical Courage

Biblical courage isn't about being fearless; it's about trusting God amidst our fears. It's having the assurance of Hebrews 11:1 (ESV) in our hearts: "Now faith is the assurance of things hoped for, the conviction of things not seen."

The Old Testament story of Joshua provides a vivid example of such faith-based courage. Before entering the Promised Land, Joshua receives this divine exhortation, "Have I not commanded you? Be strong and courageous. Do not be frightened, and do not be dismayed, for the LORD your God is with you wherever you go." (Joshua 1:9, ASV)

The Trials We Face

Every believer encounters trials in their journey. Trials in the Christian context are not punishments; instead, they are situations that test our faith and allegiance to Christ. These can include personal loss, illness, persecution for faith, or moral dilemmas. They may vary in intensity and duration, but the common factor is the challenge they pose to our faith.

Unwavering Faith in the Midst of Trials

The Apostle James presents a perspective on trials that can seem paradoxical. He writes, "Count it all joy, my brothers, when you meet trials of various kinds, for you know that the testing of your faith produces steadfastness." (James 1:2-3, ESV)

The call here isn't to celebrate the trials themselves but to recognize what God can accomplish through them. Trials, while challenging, provide an opportunity for the development of steadfast faith and spiritual maturity.

Cultivating Unwavering Faith

The question then arises: how can we cultivate such unwavering faith? The following are some strategies based on biblical teachings:

Stay Rooted in the Word: Regular engagement with Scripture can remind us of God's promises and faithfulness, providing strength during trials.

Cultivate a Prayerful Attitude: Prayer is not only a means to ask for help; it is also a way to express our trust in God. It helps us to maintain our focus on God during trials.

Foster Christian Community: Fellowship with other believers can provide encouragement and practical support during difficult times.

Embrace Hope: Christian hope is not wishful thinking; it is a confident expectation based on God's promises. This hope can sustain us even in the toughest trials.

Living Out Our Faith

When we exercise unwavering faith during trials, we make a powerful statement about the reality and goodness of God. Our ability to remain steadfast under pressure can draw others to Christ and encourage fellow believers.

Consider the Apostle Paul, who faced numerous trials but remained firm in his faith, as he proclaimed in 2 Timothy 4:7 (ESV), "I have fought the good fight, I have finished the race, I have kept the faith."

Conclusion: The Blessings of Unwavering Faith

Trials are inevitable in our faith journey, but they don't have to defeat us. As we rely on God's strength and promise, we can demonstrate unwavering faith that not only sustains us but also influences others for Christ.

Remember Peter's encouragement: "In this you rejoice, though now for a little while, if necessary, you have been grieved by various trials, so that the tested genuineness of your faith... may be found to result in praise and glory and honor at the revelation of Jesus Christ." (1 Peter 1:6-7, ESV)

An unwavering faith, marked by courage, is a beacon in a world that often feels adrift, showing the way towards the ultimate harbor, our Lord Jesus Christ.

Empowering Others through Faith

The Christian faith, rooted in the life, death, and resurrection of Jesus Christ, has transformative power. This power extends beyond our personal lives, empowering us to positively impact others. This chapter discusses how our faith can empower others, becoming a catalyst for spiritual growth and transformation.

The Interconnectedness of the Christian Community

The New Testament repeatedly emphasizes the interconnectedness of believers. Apostle Paul, in his first letter to the Corinthians, uses the metaphor of a body to describe the Church, "For just as the body is one and has many members, and all the members of the body, though many, are one body, so it is with Christ." (1 Corinthians 12:12, ESV)

Each member of the body has a role and a function. So it is with us as Christians. We are called to support and empower each other in our spiritual journeys.

Empowering Others: The Biblical Perspective

Biblically, empowering others is not about exerting power over them but about serving them in love. In fact, Jesus overturned the traditional concept of power, saying, "whoever would be great among you must be your servant." (Matthew 20:26, ESV)

Empowering others through faith involves:

1. **Sharing the Gospel:** The message of salvation through Christ is the most empowering message one can share. It provides a new perspective on life and eternity, transforming the lives of those who accept it.
2. **Teaching and Discipleship:** Through teaching and discipleship, we can help others understand and apply biblical truth in their lives, leading to spiritual growth and maturity.
3. **Spiritual Encouragement:** Words of faith and encouragement can bolster others' spirits, helping them persevere through trials and remain steadfast in their faith.
4. **Prayer:** Intercessory prayer is a powerful way to support others. It acknowledges our dependence on God's power and seeks His intervention in others' lives.

Biblical Examples of Empowering Others

The Bible is replete with examples of individuals who empowered others through their faith. Consider Barnabas, who was known for his encouragement. He empowered Paul, standing by him when others were doubtful of his conversion. He also empowered John Mark by giving him a second chance when Paul had given up on him (Acts 15:36-39, ESV). Barnabas' actions led to the spiritual growth of these individuals and the spread of the Gospel.

The Impact of Empowering Others

Empowering others through faith doesn't only benefit those who receive it; it also enriches our own faith journey. It strengthens our relationship with God, deepens our understanding of His Word, and develops our character.

Moreover, empowering others creates a positive ripple effect in the Christian community, promoting unity, mutual growth, and the collective witness of the Church.

Conclusion: The Call to Empower Others

As followers of Christ, we are called to empower others through faith. As the Apostle Peter urged, "As each has received a gift, use it to serve one another, as good stewards of God's varied grace." (1 Peter 4:10, ESV)

By empowering others, we live out our faith courageously, tangibly expressing God's love and advancing His Kingdom. In doing so, we make a profound difference in the lives of others and in our spiritual communities, reaffirming that we, as individuals, can and do make a significant difference.

Courage, the Catalyst for Change

Faith and courage are inseparable. To truly live out the Christian faith is to act with courage, not because of personal strength, but because of the confidence that comes from knowing and trusting in God. This chapter will delve into how courage, fueled by faith, can be a catalyst for change in our lives and in the lives of others.

Understanding Courage

At its core, courage is not about fearlessness. It is about stepping forward in the face of fear because you believe in something greater than the fear itself. In the Christian context, courage is about taking action in faith, trusting in God's promises and provision. This is beautifully encapsulated in the words of the Psalmist, "The Lord is my light and my salvation; whom shall I fear? The Lord is the stronghold of my life; of whom shall I be afraid?" (Psalm 27:1, ESV)

Courage in the Life of a Believer

Courage is crucial in a believer's life. Here's why:

1. **Standing Firm in Faith:** It takes courage to hold on to faith in a world that often contradicts Christian values. This was evident in the life of Daniel who, despite the decree of King Darius, chose to openly pray to God, risking his life in the process (Daniel 6, ESV).

2. **Spreading the Gospel:** Sharing the Gospel message requires courage. It involves stepping out of our comfort zones and risking rejection. However, as Paul states in Romans 1:16 (ESV), "For I am not ashamed of the gospel, for it is the power of God for salvation to everyone who believes."

3. **Serving Others:** Serving others, especially those who are marginalized or disadvantaged, demands courage. It involves personal sacrifice and sometimes, confrontation with societal norms and structures.

Courage as a Catalyst for Change

Courageous action, driven by faith, can bring about significant change. The biblical narrative is replete with such instances.

Consider the courage of Moses, who, despite his initial reluctance, led the Israelites out of Egyptian bondage (Exodus 3-14, ESV). Or think of Esther, who risked her life to save her people from annihilation (Esther 4-7, ESV). In both instances, their courage fueled by faith resulted in significant changes.

The Call to Courageous Faith

Courage is not a trait reserved for a select few. As believers, we are all called to courageous faith. Ephesians 6:10 (ESV) exhorts us to "be strong in the Lord and in the strength of his might."

The Bible also provides us with practical guidance on cultivating courage:

1. **Immerse in the Word of God:** The Bible is a rich resource for understanding God's character, promises, and His faithfulness throughout history. It reinforces our faith and bolsters our courage.

2. **Pray:** Through prayer, we can seek God's wisdom, strength, and guidance. It is a space where we can lay our fears before God and receive His peace.

3. **Lean on Christian Community:** A supportive Christian community can encourage us, share our burdens, and provide wise counsel.

Conclusion: The Courage to Make a Difference

Courageous faith can truly make a difference – it changes us, and through us, it can change the world. As we face challenges, let's remember Joshua's commission: "Have I not commanded you? Be strong and courageous. Do not be frightened, and do not be dismayed, for the Lord your God is with you wherever you go." (Joshua 1:9, ESV)

Through our courageous faith in action, we bear witness to the power and love of God, becoming catalysts for change and making a profound difference in the world.

CHAPTER 6 Making a Difference Through Service

Serving With a Purpose: The Christian Mission

Service is central to the Christian life. It is a tangible expression of love, compassion, and commitment to the principles of the Gospel. As Christians, we are called to serve with purpose, aligning our actions with the greater Christian mission. This chapter will explore this concept in greater depth, underlining the importance of service as a means of making a difference.

The Biblical Mandate of Service

Scripture is replete with the exhortation to serve. The ministry of Jesus provides the perfect example of servanthood. In Mark 10:45 (ESV), Jesus states, "For even the Son of Man did not come to be served, but to serve, and to give his life as a ransom for many." In this statement, we find not just an example but a call for all believers to emulate Jesus' servant leadership.

Similarly, the Apostle Paul in Galatians 5:13 (ESV) urges believers to, "through love serve one another." Clearly, the biblical mandate for service is unequivocal.

Serving with Purpose: The Christian Mission

Every act of service should have a purpose that is in alignment with the Christian mission. But what is this mission?

The Christian mission is best encapsulated in the Great Commission (Matthew 28:19-20, ESV), where Jesus instructs his followers to "Go therefore and make disciples of all nations, baptizing them in the name of the Father and of the Son and of the Holy Spirit, teaching them to observe all that I have commanded you."

The mission, therefore, has two dimensions:

1. **Evangelism:** Sharing the Gospel and making disciples is a central part of the Christian mission. It involves speaking about God's love, grace, and the redeeming work of Jesus Christ.
2. **Discipleship:** Teaching others to observe Jesus' commandments involves modeling a Christ-like life and helping others grow in their faith. It includes acts of love, mercy, justice, and service.

Making a Difference Through Service

Service is not just about doing good for others; it is about bringing them closer to God. When we serve others selflessly, we mirror God's love, opening doors for others to experience His grace. Here's how we can make a difference:

1. **Meet Physical Needs:** As Christians, we are called to care for the physical needs of others, as seen in Matthew 25:35-36 (ESV) where Jesus speaks about feeding the hungry, giving drink to the thirsty, welcoming the stranger, clothing the naked, and visiting the sick and imprisoned.
2. **Meet Emotional Needs:** Service also involves meeting emotional needs by offering comfort, encouragement, and support to those in distress.
3. **Meet Spiritual Needs:** Ultimately, service should aim to meet spiritual needs by sharing the Gospel and discipling others.

Serving Faithfully

While serving, it's crucial to remember:

1. **Serve Selflessly:** Christian service is about putting others before self, as Jesus did.
2. **Serve Humbly:** Humility is key to Christian service. We serve not for recognition, but out of love for God and others.
3. **Serve Diligently:** Diligence in service means doing our best and being faithful in all tasks, big or small.

4. **Serve in Unity:** We are called to serve together as the body of Christ, valuing each other's gifts and roles.

Conclusion: The Impact of Service

Serving with a purpose enables us to be effective agents of change in the world. It helps meet immediate needs, demonstrates God's love in practical ways, and contributes to the spiritual growth of others. By faithfully serving others, we can truly make a difference, living out the Christian mission in a world that so desperately needs to see the love and grace of Christ.

Tangible Love: Caring for the Least of These

In the Christian journey, our mission is to express our faith through actions that reflect God's love. One of the most profound ways we can do this is by caring for 'the least of these'. This phrase originates from Matthew 25:40 (ESV), where Jesus tells His disciples, "Truly, I say to you, as you did it to one of the least of these my brothers, you did it to me."

Who are 'the Least of These'?

In Jesus' teachings, 'the least of these' often refers to individuals marginalized by society due to poverty, illness, or other unfortunate circumstances. They represent individuals most in need of love, care, and support – be it the hungry, thirsty, stranger, naked, sick, or those in prison, as mentioned in Matthew 25:35-36 (ESV).

The Biblical Call to Care

Scripture calls us to care for 'the least of these' repeatedly, underscoring the importance of our responsibility toward them.

In the Old Testament, Proverbs 31:8-9 (ASV) states, "Open thy mouth for the dumb, in the cause of all such as are left desolate. Open thy mouth, judge righteously, and minister justice to the poor and needy." This verse underscores our duty to advocate for those who cannot advocate for themselves, further emphasizing the call to service.

In the New Testament, 1 John 3:17-18 (ESV) asks, "But if anyone has the world's goods and sees his brother in need, yet closes his heart against him, how does God's love abide in him? Little children, let us not love in word or talk but in deed and in truth." This reinforces the need for active, tangible expressions of love towards others.

Caring for 'the Least of These' in Practice

Caring for 'the least of these' involves practical actions that meet real needs. Here's how we can put this into practice:

1. **Feed the Hungry:** This could involve donating to food banks, supporting hunger relief organizations, or volunteering to distribute meals to those in need.
2. **Clothe the Naked:** Donating clothes to those who need them is a simple yet effective way to meet a basic human need.
3. **Shelter the Stranger:** This might mean supporting organizations that provide housing for the homeless or refugees, or it could be as simple as being a welcoming presence in your community.
4. **Visit the Sick and Imprisoned:** Spend time with those who are sick, providing company, encouragement, and practical support. Also, consider prison ministry opportunities as a way of reaching out to those often forgotten by society.

The Impact of Caring

When we care for 'the least of these,' we do more than meet their immediate needs. We affirm their worth and dignity as individuals made in God's image. We demonstrate God's love in tangible ways and make a real difference in their lives. Furthermore, we follow in the footsteps of Christ, who consistently showed compassion and kindness towards the marginalized and neglected.

A Heart for 'the Least of These'

As believers, we need to develop a heart for 'the least of these.' This means seeing them through God's eyes – not as burdens to be avoided, but as people to be loved. It means letting their needs move our hearts to action. And it means realizing that in serving them, we serve Christ Himself.

Caring for 'the least of these' is not an optional extra for the Christian life. It's at the heart of our calling. As we reach out in love and service to those in need, we reflect God's heart and make a significant difference in the world around us. In doing so, we embody the Gospel, demonstrating the tangible love of Christ to a world in need.

Mobilizing for Missions: Serving Beyond Borders

When we consider serving as Christians, our minds often turn to local contexts. However, our calling to make a difference is not limited to our immediate environment. This chapter examines the significance of missions – serving beyond borders – as a crucial part of the Christian faith.

The Biblical Foundation for Missions

The idea of missions is rooted in the Bible. From the Old Testament's prophecy of a blessing for all nations through Abraham (Genesis 12:1-3 ASV) to Jesus' command to make disciples of all nations (Matthew 28:19-20 ESV), the Bible provides a strong foundation for missions.

In Acts 1:8 (ESV), Jesus instructed His disciples, "But you will receive power when the Holy Spirit has come upon you, and you will be my witnesses in Jerusalem and in all Judea and Samaria, and to the end of the earth." This verse establishes the geographical expansion of the Gospel message, starting locally and extending globally.

Understanding Missions

Missions involve sending individuals or groups across cultural boundaries to proclaim the Gospel message, disciple believers, plant churches, and serve communities in the name of Jesus. They are a powerful expression of God's heart for all people and a critical part of fulfilling the Great Commission.

Mobilizing for Missions

Mobilizing for missions requires understanding our role within the larger context of God's mission. Every Christian is called to participate in missions, whether as senders, goers, or supporters.

1. **Senders:** Not everyone is called to go to foreign lands, but we can all be senders. This involves praying for missionaries, giving financially to support their work, and promoting awareness about missions within our local churches and communities.
2. **Goers:** Some Christians are called to go into the mission field. This is a significant decision that requires much prayer, preparation, and commitment.
3. **Supporters:** Every missionary needs a support system – people who will provide encouragement, prayer, and resources. By providing this support, we share in the work of the missionaries we help.

Making a Difference Through Missions

Missions can have a profound impact both on those being served and on those serving. For those in the mission field, the work of missionaries can provide practical help, offer hope, and introduce the transformative power of the Gospel. For the missionaries, serving in this way can deepen their faith, broaden their perspectives, and connect them more deeply with God's global family.

Challenges and Rewards

Undertaking missions is not without its challenges. It may involve leaving comfort zones, facing cultural shock, and encountering physical hardships. However, the rewards are considerable. Through missions, Christians can express God's love in tangible ways, impact communities, and participate directly in the work God is doing around the world.

Conclusion

As Christians, we are called to make a difference in the world. Missions offer an avenue to extend God's love and the message of the Gospel beyond our borders. Whether we serve as senders, goers, or supporters, we each have a role to play in this grand, divine endeavor. As we mobilize for missions, we join in God's global mission and embody the Great Commission, serving as witnesses of Christ "to the end of the earth."

CHAPTER 7 Living Joyfully in Christ

The Joy of the Lord as Our Strength

The life of a Christian is not exempt from trials and tribulations. However, amidst these struggles, believers have access to a profound source of strength— the joy of the Lord. This chapter delves into the nature, source, and implications of this joy, illustrating how it can serve as our strength in all seasons of life.

Understanding the Joy of the Lord

Joy in the Biblical sense is more than a fleeting emotion or a response to favorable circumstances. It is a deep-seated assurance and contentment rooted in our relationship with God and our knowledge of His love, provision, and sovereignty.

Nehemiah 8:10 (ASV) gives us a glimpse into this joy: "…the joy of Jehovah is your strength." This verse suggests that God's joy—His delight and satisfaction—is the wellspring of our strength. This joy becomes our fortress, enabling us to weather life's challenges.

The Source of Our Joy

The foundation of our joy lies in our relationship with Christ. In John 15:11 (ESV), Jesus says, "These things I have spoken to you, that my joy may be in you, and that your joy may be full." As we abide in Christ and His words abide in us, His joy fills us.

The joy we have as Christians stems from the assurance of our salvation (Luke 10:20 ESV), the presence of the Holy Spirit (Romans 14:17 ESV), and our hope in God's promises (Romans 15:13 ESV).

The Joy of the Lord as Our Strength

Joy in the Lord is not merely a personal comfort; it is a robust source of strength that sustains us in all situations.

1. **Strength in Trials:** James 1:2-4 (ESV) instructs believers to count it all joy when we meet trials. Why? Because these trials test our faith, producing steadfastness. This is a paradoxical concept to the world, yet profound in the Kingdom of God. Our joy, rooted in God's sovereignty and goodness, gives us the strength to endure.

2. **Strength in Service:** Serving others can be challenging and draining. However, when we serve with the joy of the Lord, we find an undergirding strength. Acts 20:35 (ESV) illustrates this, quoting Jesus: "It is more blessed to give than to receive." In giving of ourselves joyfully, we draw upon the reservoir of God's strength.

3. **Strength in Evangelism:** Sharing the Gospel is a joyous task that requires courage and conviction. The joy of the Lord emboldens us to speak the truth in love, just as the apostles did in the early church, even in the face of persecution (Acts 5:41 ESV).

Living Out Joy in Christ

Living joyfully in Christ is a transformative practice. It changes our perspective, fuels our resilience, enhances our witness, and ultimately, glorifies God. Here are ways to cultivate this joy:

1. **Abide in Christ:** Maintaining a close relationship with Christ through prayer, Bible study, and obedience allows His joy to dwell in us (John 15:10-11 ESV).

2. **Foster Gratitude:** Being thankful, even in trials, shifts our focus from our circumstances to God's goodness and faithfulness, breeding joy (1 Thessalonians 5:18 ESV).

3. **Share the Joy:** Sharing our joy with others—through encouragement, sharing our testimony, and serving joyfully—multiplies this joy and strengthens our faith community (2 Corinthians 1:24 ESV).

Conclusion

The joy of the Lord is a profound, life-giving force available to all believers. It is more than a positive emotion; it is a spiritual strength, rooted in our relationship with Christ and our assurance of God's goodness and sovereignty. As we live joyfully in Christ, we tap into this strength, enabling us to endure trials, serve others, and share the Gospel with boldness and love. Truly, the joy of the Lord is our strength!

Radiating the Love of Christ

Living joyfully in Christ has a direct impact on how we express love to those around us. This chapter will delve into how our joy in Christ influences our capacity to radiate His love to others.

Understanding Christ's Love

To radiate the love of Christ, we must first grasp the depth and breadth of His love. Ephesians 3:17-19 (ESV) captures this: "…that you, being rooted and grounded in love, may have strength to comprehend with all the saints what is the breadth and length and height and depth, and to know the love of Christ that surpasses knowledge…" Christ's love is vast, sacrificial, unconditional, and redemptive.

The Joyful Life and Christ's Love

Our joy in Christ is not a self-contained experience. It naturally overflows into the expression of love. As we find our joy in Christ, His love compels us to extend this love to others.

1. **Love that Reflects Christ:** When our joy is rooted in Christ, our love for others becomes a reflection of His love. We begin to love others not out of obligation or self-interest, but from a place of genuine joy in Christ and appreciation for His love (1 John 4:19, ESV).
2. **Love that Serves:** The joy of the Lord in our hearts enables us to serve others joyfully. It's not a burdensome duty but a

joyful expression of Christ's love. Galatians 5:13 (ESV) encourages us to "...through love serve one another."

3. **Love that Sacrifices:** The love of Christ is marked by sacrifice, most notably, His sacrifice on the cross (John 15:13, ESV). Our joy in Christ gives us the strength to make sacrifices for the good of others.

Radiating the Love of Christ

To radiate the love of Christ effectively, it must first permeate our hearts and lives. This involves:

1. **Abiding in Christ's Love:** We must consistently dwell in the love of Christ, which is the source of our joy. Jesus instructs us in John 15:9 (ESV), "As the Father has loved me, so have I loved you. Abide in my love."

2. **Being Transformed by Christ's Love:** As we abide in Christ's love, it transforms us, making us more like Him. This transformation impacts how we interact with others, radiating His love through our lives (2 Corinthians 3:18, ESV).

3. **Actively Expressing Christ's Love:** Radiating Christ's love requires active expression. This could be through acts of kindness, service, forgiveness, and the sharing of the Gospel. As Matthew 5:16 (ESV) instructs, "...let your light shine before others, so that they may see your good works and give glory to your Father who is in heaven."

Conclusion

Radiating the love of Christ is a natural outflow of living joyfully in Christ. As we find our joy in Him, His love fills our hearts and spills over into our interactions with others. This is not a passive process but an active endeavor that involves abiding in Christ's love, being transformed by it, and expressing it in tangible ways. This radiant love not only impacts the lives of those we interact with but also glorifies God, the source of our joy and love. In this way, we truly make a difference in the world around us.

Fostering a Joyous Christian Community

Joy is a profound element of the Christian life and a signature trait of the Christian community. This chapter will explore the essence of fostering a joyous Christian community grounded in Christ's love.

Joy in the Christian Community

The Christian community is called to be characterized by joy. This joy is rooted not in temporal circumstances, but in the eternal reality of Christ's saving grace. As stated in Psalm 16:11 (ASV), "Thou wilt show me the path of life: In thy presence is fullness of joy; In thy right hand there are pleasures forevermore."

The Source of Our Joy

Joy is not merely a human emotion but a fruit of the Holy Spirit dwelling within believers. It arises from the knowledge of our salvation, the presence of God in our lives, and the hope we have in Jesus Christ. This divine joy is independent of our circumstances, and it sustains us even in times of trials and tribulations.

Creating a Joyous Christian Community

Fostering a joyous Christian community requires intentional effort. Here are a few key factors that can contribute to creating such an environment:

1. **Living Joyfully:** The joy of the Lord should be evident in our personal lives, reflecting in our attitudes, actions, and interactions. As Nehemiah 8:10 (ESV) states, "...the joy of the LORD is your strength."

2. **Promoting Unity:** Unity is essential in fostering a joyous community. As Christians, we are called to "...be of the same mind, having the same love, being in full accord and of one mind" (Philippians 2:2, ESV). Unity breeds joy as we collectively focus on the love of Christ and the mission of the gospel.

3. **Encouraging One Another:** Encouragement helps to foster joy in the community. Hebrews 3:13 (ESV) tells us to "...encourage one another daily...", and this mutual support helps to maintain the joy in the community, especially during challenging times.

4. **Worshipping and Praying Together:** Collective worship and prayer are powerful tools in fostering a joyous community. When we engage in these practices, we not only strengthen our relationship with God but also with each other, fostering mutual joy and edification.

Living Out Joy in Community

Having a joyous community isn't merely about having happy gatherings. It's about living out our joy in Christ in tangible ways that impact the lives of others. Here's how we can do that:

1. **Showing Love and Compassion:** Our joy in Christ should drive us to love and care for others, reflecting Christ's love and compassion (1 John 4:7, ESV).

2. **Serving Together:** Serving God and serving others are excellent ways of expressing and fostering joy. Service unites us, helps us to grow spiritually, and allows us to contribute to God's work (Galatians 5:13, ESV).

3. **Sharing the Gospel:** Sharing the Good News of Jesus Christ is one of the most joyous acts we can engage in. As we lead others to Christ, we add to the joy in heaven and within our community (Luke 15:10, ESV).

Conclusion

Creating a joyous Christian community is not an optional extra but a biblical imperative. It's about living out our joy in Christ and fostering an environment where this joy becomes contagious. By promoting unity, encouraging one another, worshipping and praying together, showing love and compassion, serving together, and sharing the Gospel, we can foster a community where the joy of the Lord truly is our strength. And in this joyous atmosphere, we can make a difference, both within the community and beyond.

CHAPTER 8 Your Personal Impact

The Power of Personal Testimony

Your personal testimony has a unique power. It encapsulates your personal journey with Christ and can serve as a powerful tool in your Christian walk and mission. This chapter will delve into the nature of personal testimonies and the impact they can have on individuals and the broader community.

Understanding Personal Testimony

In essence, your personal testimony is your Christian story. It encompasses your life before Christ, your encounter with Christ, and your life after accepting Christ. This narrative can be a powerful tool to share the Gospel, as it gives a tangible, relatable account of God's work in your life.

The Biblical Foundation of Personal Testimony

The concept of personal testimony is rooted in the Bible. The New Testament is replete with instances where individuals shared their encounters with Christ, serving as a testament to His power and grace. Perhaps one of the most dramatic of these is the Apostle Paul's conversion story, which he shared on multiple occasions to different audiences (Acts 22:1-21; Acts 26:12-18, ESV). These accounts underscore the transformative power of Christ and the value of sharing such experiences with others.

The Power of Your Personal Testimony

Your personal testimony holds a significant power for several reasons:

1. **It's Unique:** No one else has the same story as you. Your unique experiences and perspectives add a fresh dimension to the narrative of God's work.
2. **It's Personal:** Your testimony isn't an abstract theological discourse—it's a personal narrative of your encounter with Christ. This personal element can make it more relatable and impactful to the listener.
3. **It's Evidence of God's Work:** Your testimony serves as tangible proof of God's transformative power, illustrating how He works in the lives of individuals.

Sharing Your Personal Testimony

As powerful as your testimony is, it only makes a difference when you share it with others. Here are a few pointers on how you can effectively share your personal testimony:

1. **Pray for Guidance:** Before you share your testimony, pray for God's guidance. Ask Him to use your story for His glory and to prepare the hearts of those who will hear it.
2. **Be Authentic:** Share your story honestly, without exaggeration or omission. Authenticity increases the impact of your testimony.
3. **Keep Christ at the Center:** Your testimony is ultimately about Christ's work in your life. Keep Him at the center of your story, emphasizing His grace and transformative power.
4. **Be Respectful and Gentle:** Remember the words in 1 Peter 3:15 (ESV), "...Always be prepared to make a defense to anyone who asks you for a reason for the hope that is in you; yet do it with gentleness and respect..." Be considerate of the listener's beliefs and perspectives as you share your testimony.

The Impact of Your Personal Testimony

Your personal testimony can have a profound impact, both on those who hear it and on your own faith journey. It can:

1. **Lead Others to Christ:** Your testimony can help others understand the Gospel on a personal level, potentially leading them to Christ.
2. **Strengthen Your Faith:** Revisiting your faith journey can strengthen your faith, reminding you of God's faithfulness and transformative power.
3. **Encourage Other Believers:** Your testimony can encourage other believers, reminding them of God's work and helping them feel less alone in their struggles.

Conclusion

Your personal testimony is a powerful tool in your Christian journey. It allows you to share God's work in your life, encouraging others and strengthening your own faith. As such, it serves as a testament to the transformative power of Christ's love and grace.

Empowering Others through Discipleship

In the Christian walk, one of the most impactful ways you can make a difference is through discipleship. This process, as established by Jesus Himself, is a powerful means of spiritual multiplication that can significantly influence both individuals and communities.

Understanding Discipleship

Discipleship is a process that involves guiding and nurturing others in their spiritual growth and relationship with Christ. The term 'disciple' derives from the Greek word 'mathetes,' meaning 'learner' or 'student.' Thus, in a biblical context, a disciple is someone who follows and learns from Jesus.

The Biblical Mandate for Discipleship

The biblical mandate for discipleship is clear, found directly in the Great Commission where Jesus commanded His disciples: "Go therefore and make disciples of all nations, baptizing them in the name of the Father and of the Son and of the Holy Spirit, teaching them to observe all that I have commanded you." (Matthew 28:19-20, ESV). This directive was not merely for the original apostles but extends to all followers of Christ.

The Process of Discipleship

Discipleship involves three main stages: leading others to Christ, nurturing their spiritual growth, and empowering them to disciple others. This cyclical process ensures the growth and sustainability of the Christian community.

1. **Leading Others to Christ:** This is the first step in discipleship. It involves sharing the Gospel message and inviting individuals to accept Christ as their Lord and Savior.

2. **Nurturing Spiritual Growth:** After leading others to Christ, discipleship entails helping them grow in their faith. This involves teaching biblical truths, fostering spiritual disciplines, and modeling a Christ-like life.

3. **Empowering to Disciple Others:** The ultimate goal of discipleship is not just to create disciples but to make disciple-makers. As such, disciples are to be equipped and encouraged to guide others in their spiritual journeys.

The Role of the Discipler

As a discipler, your role is to guide, nurture, and empower. This requires a deep commitment to both the person you're discipling and to Christ Himself. To be effective, a discipler should be prayerful, patient, loving, and rooted in the Word of God. Additionally, you should be willing to invest time and effort, understand the individual's unique spiritual needs, and strive to model Christ in your life.

The Impact of Discipleship

Discipleship is a powerful tool for personal and community transformation:

1. **Personal Transformation:** For the disciple, discipleship fosters spiritual growth, deepens understanding of biblical truths, and enhances personal relationship with Christ.

2. **Community Transformation:** On a broader scale, discipleship leads to spiritual multiplication, resulting in a vibrant, growing Christian community. It fosters unity, mutual support, and collective spiritual growth.
3. **Global Impact:** The Great Commission's mandate of making disciples of all nations implies a global scope. Through discipleship, the Gospel can reach far corners of the world, transforming lives and communities globally.

Conclusion

Discipleship, at its core, is about living out Christ's love and teachings and guiding others to do the same. It is a lifelong journey that involves continual learning, growth, and sharing. Through discipleship, we not only grow personally but also empower others, leading to a ripple effect that can transform communities and ultimately, the world for Christ. Remember, the discipleship journey is not meant to be walked alone. As you empower others through discipleship, you also make a significant difference in the spread and depth of the Christian faith.

Making a Difference, One Person at a Time

When contemplating the grand scope of humanity and the issues the world faces, it can be overwhelming to consider how a single individual could make a difference. Yet, the Bible offers us countless examples of individuals whose faith and actions had monumental impacts on their communities and even the course of history. You, too, can make a difference, one person at a time.

The Biblical Model

In the New Testament, we find several instances where Jesus engaged with individuals, recognizing their unique needs and worth. The woman at the well (John 4:1-26, ESV), Zacchaeus the tax collector (Luke 19:1-10, ESV), and the thief on the cross (Luke 23:39-43, ESV) are just a few examples of Jesus' individual encounters. In each instance, Jesus' interactions resulted in life-changing transformations for these individuals, with ripple effects that extended far beyond their personal experiences.

The Power of One

At first glance, making a difference in one person's life may seem insignificant, but it's essential to understand the power of one. Each individual's influence extends to their family, friends, and community. Therefore, when we impact one life positively, it can have a domino effect, influencing countless other lives indirectly.

One-on-One Ministry

Making a difference one person at a time often involves engaging in one-on-one ministry. This type of ministry can take various forms, such as mentoring, discipleship, or simple friendship, but the focus is always on meeting individual needs and demonstrating Christ's love and care.

This approach does not require extraordinary abilities or resources. Instead, it requires a heart that is sensitive to the Holy Spirit's leading, a willingness to be present and listen, and a readiness to respond in love and truth to the needs presented.

Practical Steps for One-on-One Impact

Here are some practical steps you can take to start making a difference one person at a time:

1. **Pray:** Prayer is foundational in all Christian endeavors. Ask God to direct you to the individuals He wants you to impact. Pray also for the wisdom, sensitivity, and boldness to minister effectively to their needs.

2. **Connect:** Building relationships is key to making an impact. Engage with people in your sphere of influence — family, friends, colleagues, neighbors. Show genuine interest in their lives, and strive to create a safe, trusting environment for them.

3. **Share:** As you build relationships, opportunities will naturally arise for you to share your faith and experiences with Christ.

Do this gently and respectfully, always mindful of the person's readiness to hear and respond.

4. **Serve:** Actions often speak louder than words. Demonstrating Christ's love through acts of kindness and service can have a profound impact on people and open doors for deeper spiritual discussions.

Conclusion

Jesus taught us that every individual has immense worth in God's eyes. He cared deeply for each person He met, recognizing their unique value and potential. We are called to do the same — to see the individuals within the crowd and to impact their lives with the love and truth of Christ.

Making a difference one person at a time may seem like a small endeavor, but in God's kingdom, nothing is insignificant. The ripple effect of impacting one life can lead to transformation in families, communities, and even generations. Remember, the greatest impact often comes not from grand gestures but from humble, consistent acts of love and faithfulness.

CHAPTER 9 Embracing Your Role as a Difference Maker

The Power of Small Gestures

In the grand scheme of things, small gestures may appear inconsequential. Yet, when embraced with a sincere heart and the guiding light of Christ, these gestures can bring forth immense power, ultimately leading to significant changes in the lives of others. This chapter aims to guide you on how to embrace your role as a difference maker by harnessing the power of small gestures.

Understanding the Power of Small Gestures

In the Gospel of Matthew, Jesus uses the parable of the mustard seed (Matthew 13:31-32, ESV) to illustrate how something small can grow into something remarkably large. The same principle applies to our actions: even small gestures of kindness, love, and compassion can have a profound impact, often greater than we could ever imagine.

Small Gestures in the Bible

The Bible is filled with examples of small gestures making significant impacts. The widow's mite (Luke 21:1-4, ESV), the cup of cold water (Matthew 10:42, ESV), and Dorcas' acts of kindness (Acts 9:36-42, ESV) are instances that highlight the power of small gestures. These seemingly insignificant acts borne out of sincere hearts created ripples of influence, demonstrating that size does not determine significance in the kingdom of God.

Embracing Your Role as a Difference Maker

The first step towards embracing your role as a difference maker is to recognize and accept that you, as a follower of Christ, are indeed called to make a difference in the world. This understanding changes your perspective, allowing you to see opportunities for service in everyday situations.

Moreover, the power of small gestures lies in their authenticity. These acts are not about grandeur or recognition but about genuinely demonstrating Christ's love. As you embrace your role, remember to perform these gestures with sincere love and humility, reflecting the nature of Jesus who "came not to be served but to serve" (Mark 10:45, ESV).

The Impact of Small Gestures

Small gestures can make a big difference in several ways. They can uplift spirits, foster community, build relationships, and reflect God's love. Through these acts, we not only extend Christ's love to others but also strengthen our spiritual growth as we embody Christ's servant leadership.

Practical Ways to Make a Difference

Here are some practical ways you can make a difference through small gestures:

1. **Prayer:** One of the most powerful yet overlooked gestures is prayer. Praying for others—be it their wellbeing, struggles, or spiritual growth—is a potent gesture of love and concern.

2. **Acts of Kindness:** Simple acts of kindness, such as helping a neighbor, providing a meal, or giving an encouraging word, can have a significant impact.

3. **Presence:** Sometimes, the best gift you can give someone is your presence. Being there for someone, listening to their worries, and offering comfort can make a huge difference in their life.

4. **Use Your Gifts:** God has blessed each of us with unique talents and abilities. Use your God-given gifts to serve others, no matter how small it might seem.

Conclusion

The world often measures success in terms of scale and grandeur, but God's kingdom operates differently. In God's eyes, the small gestures made in love and obedience can yield great fruit.

Embrace your role as a difference maker. Never underestimate the power of small gestures performed in love. Let us remember the words of Mother Teresa: "Not all of us can do great things. But we can do small things with great love." In this way, we can impact the world around us, one small gesture at a time, for the glory of God.

Balancing Responsibility with Grace

As Christians, we are called to live out our faith in a way that makes a positive difference in the world around us. This call comes with the responsibility to act with love and compassion. However, in our zeal to fulfill our role as difference makers, it is vital to balance our responsibilities with grace. This chapter will explore how to maintain this balance in our pursuit of embodying the love of Christ in our daily interactions.

Understanding Responsibility and Grace

Before we can balance responsibility with grace, we must understand what these terms mean in a biblical context.

Responsibility in the Christian context refers to our duties or obligations as followers of Christ. We are responsible for living out the commands and teachings of Christ, which include loving our neighbors, practicing forgiveness, and seeking justice.

Grace, on the other hand, is the unmerited favor of God. It is His loving-kindness and mercy, given freely to us, not because we have earned it, but because God desires to give it. Grace reminds us that while we strive to fulfill our responsibilities, we are saved not by our actions, but by the love and sacrifice of Jesus Christ.

The Biblical Basis for Responsibility and Grace

Both responsibility and grace are foundational elements of Christian faith. The Bible teaches us about our responsibilities as followers of Christ. For example, in Matthew 22:39 (ESV), Jesus commands us to "Love your neighbor as yourself," illustrating our responsibility towards others.

Simultaneously, the Bible is abundant with references to God's grace. Ephesians 2:8-9 (ESV) tells us, "For by grace you have been saved through faith. And this is not your own doing; it is the gift of God, not a result of works, so that no one may boast."

Balancing Responsibility with Grace

Balancing responsibility with grace is a delicate act. It involves earnestly striving to fulfill our Christian duties, while also recognizing that we are bound to fall short. It is here that grace comes into play. Grace doesn't absolve us from our responsibilities, but it does provide us comfort and reassurance that our salvation is not dependent on our perfect fulfillment of these duties.

It is important to remember that our efforts to make a difference should not be driven by guilt or a desire to earn God's favor. Instead, they should stem from our gratitude for His grace and our love for Him. When we act out of love and gratitude, our actions are not burdensome but joyful, and we reflect the grace we have received onto others.

Living Responsibly with Grace

Here are practical ways to live responsibly with grace:

1. **Practice Humility:** Acknowledge that all we do is not by our strength but through God's grace (1 Corinthians 15:10, ESV). This keeps us grounded and helps us not to become self-righteous in our actions.

2. **Embrace Imperfection:** We are human, and we will make mistakes. Instead of being disheartened when we fall short, let's use these moments as opportunities to experience God's grace anew.

3. **Extend Grace to Others:** Just as we receive grace from God, we are to extend grace to others. Be patient, forgiving, and loving towards those around us, even when it's challenging.

Conclusion

Balancing responsibility with grace is an integral part of embracing our role as difference makers. As we live out our Christian responsibilities, let's always remember the grace that has been bestowed upon us through Christ. Our responsibility to make a difference is a response to God's grace, not a means to earn it. In this understanding lies the true freedom and joy of serving as Christ's ambassadors in the world.

Building a Legacy of Love and Faith

In the journey of faith, every Christian has the potential to leave a legacy - a lasting impact that extends beyond our lifetime. This legacy isn't about monuments or material wealth; rather, it's a legacy of love and faith. This chapter will delve into understanding the importance of building such a legacy and provide guidance on how to do so.

Understanding the Concept of a Legacy of Love and Faith

A legacy of love and faith is the enduring impact of a Christian life well-lived. It is seen in the lives touched, the faith inspired, and the love demonstrated to others. This kind of legacy has eternal value, echoing in the words of Jesus in Matthew 22:37-40 (ESV), which encapsulates our Christian responsibility to love God and our neighbor.

The Biblical Basis for a Legacy of Love and Faith

The Bible is replete with examples of individuals who left a lasting legacy of love and faith. The Apostle Paul, in his second letter to Timothy, refers to the sincere faith that first dwelt in Timothy's grandmother Lois and his mother Eunice, which was now evident in Timothy as well (2 Timothy 1:5, ESV). Here, we see a multi-generational legacy of faith.

How to Build a Legacy of Love and Faith

Building a legacy of love and faith isn't achieved overnight. It is the culmination of daily acts of faithfulness, love, and service. Here are some practical ways to do this:

1. **Love Unconditionally:** Demonstrate God's love through your actions. This includes loving the unlovable, just as God loves us despite our flaws (Romans 5:8, ESV).

2. **Live Your Faith:** Ensure your life aligns with the principles of your faith. Actions often speak louder than words, so living a life of integrity is crucial.
3. **Invest in People:** Pour love and faith into the people around you. This could be through discipleship, mentoring, or simply being there for someone in need.
4. **Serve Selflessly:** Serving others is a practical way of showing love and embodying faith. Find ways to serve within your community and beyond.
5. **Pray Continually:** Prayer is a vital part of a Christian's life. It can shape us, guide us, and impact the lives of others.

Living a Life That Matters

In our quest to build a legacy of love and faith, it's important to remember that it's not about earning salvation or favor from God. Rather, it's about honoring God with our lives, serving others, and making an eternal impact.

Legacy Isn't about Fame

Often, people conflate legacy with fame or recognition. However, in God's perspective, the most influential legacies are those marked by faithfulness, love, and service. Many unnamed and unrecognized believers have left profound legacies of faith.

Leaving a Legacy for Future Generations

Our legacy of love and faith isn't just about the here and now; it's also about the impact we can have on future generations. Our actions and choices can shape the faith journeys of those who come after us, like Timothy's mother and grandmother influenced his faith.

Conclusion

Embracing our role as difference makers involves recognizing the potential for our lives to leave a lasting impact. By choosing to build a legacy of love and faith, we can affect change in our world, inspire others in their faith journeys, and honor God with our lives. This is a worthy goal for every believer and a profound way to truly make a difference.

CHAPTER 10 The Journey of a Difference Maker

Celebrating Victories, Big and Small

As difference makers in the kingdom of God, we are on a remarkable journey filled with challenges and victories, big and small. Every step we take towards making a difference counts and is worth celebrating. In this chapter, we'll delve into understanding why it's essential to celebrate victories and how we can incorporate this practice into our Christian journey.

Understanding the Significance of Celebrating Victories

Victories in our journey of faith aren't just about big milestones; they're also about the small, seemingly insignificant steps we take in obedience and faith. When we celebrate victories, we're acknowledging God's faithfulness, power, and work in and through us.

Scripture affirms the importance of rejoicing and giving thanks. In 1 Thessalonians 5:16-18 (ESV), the Apostle Paul instructs us to "Rejoice always, pray without ceasing, give thanks in all circumstances; for this is the will of God in Christ Jesus for you." Each victory, big or small, is a reason to rejoice and give thanks.

Celebrating Big Victories

Big victories may involve significant breakthroughs in our Christian journey, such as leading someone to Christ, overcoming a long-standing challenge through faith, or seeing the fruit of our ministry efforts. These victories are indeed cause for celebration.

Celebrating big victories can involve sharing the testimony with your church community, spending time in thanksgiving and praise, or even marking the occasion in a special way.

Celebrating Small Victories

Small victories are the everyday wins that might go unnoticed if we're not careful. They could be as simple as choosing to respond with love in a difficult situation, making time for daily prayer and Bible study, or extending help to a neighbor in need.

Don't overlook these victories. Celebrating them not only honors God but also builds our faith and encourages perseverance. It reminds us that our daily choices matter in God's kingdom.

The Role of Community in Celebrating Victories

We're not meant to walk our faith journey alone. The Christian community plays a vital role in celebrating victories. Sharing and celebrating our wins with fellow believers not only strengthens our own faith but also inspires and encourages others.

Victories as Testimonies

Every victory is a testament to God's faithfulness and power. By celebrating and sharing our victories, we're essentially sharing a testimony of what God has done. This can be a powerful means of encouraging others and glorifying God.

Celebrating Victories in the Midst of Challenges

Even in the midst of trials and challenges, there are victories to celebrate. Perhaps it's the peace you experience amidst turmoil or the strength to persevere in difficult circumstances. These victories remind us that God is with us even in the valleys.

Conclusion

The journey of a difference maker is marked by victories, big and small. As we faithfully walk this journey, let's remember to celebrate each victory, recognizing God's hand at work, and inspiring others to press on in their faith. After all, every victory is a testament to the fact that through Christ, we can indeed make a difference.

Looking Ahead: Your Ongoing Journey as a Difference Maker

The journey of making a difference in the world as a Christian is not a one-time event but a lifetime commitment. It's an ongoing process of learning, growing, and maturing in faith, continually seeking God's will, and being responsive to His leading. As we look forward to the path that lies ahead, it is essential to reflect on the principles that will guide us in our continuous journey as difference makers.

Perseverance in the Journey

The journey of a difference maker is often filled with challenges and obstacles. As stated in Hebrews 12:1 (ESV), we are to "run with endurance the race that is set before us." Perseverance is essential as we face trials, and we must remember to cling to the promises of God's Word and rely on His strength to carry us through.

Continual Growth and Learning

Our spiritual growth should never stagnate. As difference makers, we are called to continually grow in the knowledge of God's Word and to deepen our relationship with Him. 2 Peter 3:18 (ESV) encourages us to "grow in the grace and knowledge of our Lord and Savior Jesus Christ." Continual growth and learning help us stay grounded in our faith and equipped to serve effectively.

Maintaining a Servant's Heart

As we continue our journey, we must strive to keep a servant's heart, following the example of Jesus, who came "not to be served but to serve" (Mark 10:45, ESV). Maintaining a servant's heart means putting others' needs before ours and doing everything in love.

Remaining Flexible to God's Leading

As we forge ahead on our journey, we must remain open to God's leading, even when it means changing our plans or stepping out of our comfort zones. As Proverbs 16:9 (ESV) reminds us, "The heart of man plans his way, but the LORD establishes his steps." We must be ready to follow wherever God leads us.

Staying Connected with the Body of Christ

The Christian journey is not meant to be walked alone. Staying connected with the body of Christ – our fellow believers – is critical for mutual encouragement, accountability, and spiritual growth. "And let us consider how to stir up one another to love and good works, not neglecting to meet together" (Hebrews 10:24-25, ESV).

Keeping the Faith

In every season, keeping the faith is vital. We must hold fast to our faith in Christ, grounded in the hope of His promises. As Paul encouraged Timothy, we, too, must "fight the good fight of the faith" (1 Timothy 6:12, ESV).

Conclusion

Being a difference maker is a continuous journey of faith, hope, and love. As we look ahead, we must be prepared to face trials with perseverance, to keep growing in our knowledge of God, to maintain a servant's heart, to remain open to God's leading, and to stay connected with our fellow believers. As we journey onward, let's keep our eyes fixed on Jesus, our ultimate Difference Maker, and let His love and grace motivate us to make a difference in the world around us.

APPENDIX A Breaking Free from Negative Patterns: Renewing Your Mind in Christ

Recognizing Negative Patterns

Identifying Harmful Patterns of Thinking and Behavior

Many of us find ourselves entangled in negative patterns of thinking and behavior that we struggle to break free from. This isn't surprising given the sinful nature of humanity, but through Christ, we have the means to renew our minds and live in accordance with God's Word.

Recognizing Negative Patterns

Recognizing harmful patterns of thinking and behavior is the first step towards renewal. Negative patterns can manifest in various ways such as constant worrying, negative self-talk, grudge-holding, continual disobedience to God's commands, or even persistent sin in our lives. These patterns often have deep roots and can be challenging to identify because they have become so ingrained in our daily lives.

Paul, in his letter to the Romans, clearly stated, "Do not be conformed to this world, but be transformed by the renewal of your mind, that by testing you may discern what is the will of God, what is good and acceptable and perfect." (Romans 12:2, ESV). This transformation necessitates first recognizing that our thoughts and behaviors are not in alignment with God's will.

As believers, we have a standard by which we can measure our thoughts and actions - the Holy Bible. God's Word serves as our ultimate truth and moral compass. For example, Philippians 4:8 (ESV) tells us, "Finally, brothers, whatever is true, whatever is honorable, whatever is just, whatever is pure, whatever is lovely, whatever is commendable, if there is any excellence, if there is anything worthy of praise, think about these things." If our thoughts don't line up with these criteria, we can identify them as negative patterns.

Once we recognize our negative patterns, the next step is identifying the harmful aspects of these patterns. Often, these harmful patterns originate from false beliefs or misconceptions about ourselves, others, or God. Identifying these lies is crucial for us to reject them and replace them with God's truth.

In the Old Testament, the people of Israel repeatedly fell into cycles of disobedience, judgment, repentance, and deliverance. Their negative patterns were driven by their disobedience to God's commands and their worship of false gods. This is detailed in Judges 2:19 (ASV), "But it came to pass, when the judge was dead, that they turned back, and dealt more corruptly than their fathers, in following other gods to serve them, and to bow down unto them; they ceased not from their doings, nor from their stubborn way." This serves as a clear warning about the consequences of harmful patterns of thinking and behavior.

Renewing our minds requires the hard work of identifying these falsehoods and replacing them with God's truths. If we believe lies about ourselves, we must counter them with the truth of our identity in Christ. For example, if we struggle with feelings of worthlessness, we must remind ourselves that we are "fearfully and wonderfully made" (Psalm 139:14, ASV) and that we are God's "workmanship, created in Christ Jesus for good works, which God prepared beforehand, that we should walk in them" (Ephesians 2:10, ESV).

In conclusion, breaking free from negative patterns requires recognizing these patterns, identifying their harmful aspects, and replacing the lies driving them with God's truths. This process can be challenging and ongoing, but the promise found in Christ is one of transformation and renewal, enabling us to make a difference in our lives and those around us.

Understanding the Impact of These Patterns on Your Life

Understanding the impact of negative patterns on your life is crucial to breaking free from them. These patterns can affect us emotionally, spiritually, and even physically. They can hinder our relationships, our growth, and our faith. These negative patterns act as stumbling blocks on our path to living an abundant life in Christ.

First, these patterns can significantly impact our emotional well-being. Consistent negative thoughts, fears, or guilt can lead to stress, anxiety, and depression. It may also rob us of the joy and peace promised in the Gospel. As stated in John 14:27 (ESV), Jesus Christ assured His followers, "Peace I leave with you; my peace I give to you. Not as the world gives do I give to you. Let not your hearts be troubled, neither let them be afraid." The presence of chronic negative patterns can obstruct this divine peace from permeating our lives.

Secondly, negative patterns can hinder our spiritual growth. As followers of Christ, we are called to grow in our faith, becoming more like Jesus. However, persistent sin, constant negativity, or ingrained worldly attitudes can create a barrier in our relationship with God, stunting our spiritual growth. The Apostle Peter advised, "Like newborn infants, long for the pure spiritual milk, that by it you may grow up into salvation," (1 Peter 2:2, ESV). Negative patterns can hinder us from longing for this spiritual nourishment and growing in our salvation.

Lastly, these patterns can even impact our physical health. The stress and anxiety that often accompany these patterns can lead to various health problems such as heart disease, high blood pressure, and a weakened immune system. Proverbs 17:22 (ASV) wisely states, "A cheerful heart is a good medicine; But a broken spirit drieth up the bones." Chronic negativity can contribute to a "broken spirit," which in turn may lead to physical ailments.

But there is hope. By understanding the impact of these patterns, we can actively work to change them. Through the renewal of our minds in Christ, we can start replacing these harmful patterns with positive, Christ-centered ones. As Paul wrote in 2 Corinthians 5:17

(ESV), "Therefore, if anyone is in Christ, he is a new creation. The old has passed away; behold, the new has come." As we break free from these negative patterns, we start to see this new creation in ourselves, resulting in healthier, more Christ-centered lives that make a true difference.

Through this understanding, we can more effectively engage in the hard work of breaking these patterns and step into the fullness of life God offers us. We don't have to be bound by these negative patterns. By leaning into the transformative power of Christ, we can break free and truly make a difference.

Understanding the Power of Renewing Your Mind

Exploring the Transformative Power of Renewing Your Mind in Christ

The transformative power of renewing your mind in Christ is an exceptional element of the Christian faith. It is this renewal, this transformation, that equips us to combat and overcome the negative patterns that entangle our lives.

In his letter to the Ephesians, Paul urges believers to shed their old self, characterized by its deceitful desires, and to "be renewed in the spirit of your minds, and to put on the new self, created after the likeness of God in true righteousness and holiness." (Ephesians 4:23-24, ESV). The transformation through Christ isn't merely a change in habits or thoughts. It's the fundamental alteration of our very nature, aligning us more closely with the likeness of God.

The power of this transformation cannot be underestimated. Here are a few ways in which renewing our mind in Christ can impact our lives:

1. **Overcoming Sin**: Renewing our mind in Christ empowers us to overcome sinful patterns. Romans 6:11 (ESV) encourages us, "So you also must consider yourselves dead to sin and alive

to God in Christ Jesus." Recognizing our new identity in Christ helps us to resist sin and live in obedience to God's commands.

2. **Promoting Peace**: Renewal in Christ promotes peace in our lives. As we align our thoughts with God's truth, our anxieties and fears are replaced with His peace. Paul writes, "And the peace of God, which surpasses all understanding, will guard your hearts and your minds in Christ Jesus" (Philippians 4:7, ESV).

3. **Strengthening Faith**: The process of renewal strengthens our faith. As we continually seek to understand and apply God's Word, our faith in Him grows. The author of Hebrews asserts that "faith comes by hearing, and hearing through the word of Christ" (Hebrews 10:17, ESV). By renewing our minds with His Word, we fortify our faith.

4. **Improving Relationships**: When our minds are renewed in Christ, our relationships with others improve. The traits of love, patience, kindness, forgiveness, and humility, as outlined in 1 Corinthians 13 (ESV), become more evident in our lives, enabling us to better love and serve those around us.

5. **Cultivating Hope**: The transformation brought about by the renewal of our minds cultivates hope. As we understand more of God's character and His promises, hope blossoms within us. Romans 15:13 (ESV) says, "May the God of hope fill you with all joy and peace in believing, so that by the power of the Holy Spirit you may abound in hope."

In conclusion, the transformative power of renewing your mind in Christ is significant. It helps us break free from negative patterns, encourages personal growth, and fosters an abundant Christian life that truly makes a difference. When we engage in this renewal process, we step into a new level of faith, leaving behind the old self and fully embracing the new creation we are in Christ.

Recognizing the Importance of Aligning Your Thoughts with God's Truth

Aligning our thoughts with God's truth is crucial in the process of renewing our minds and breaking free from negative patterns. This alignment is more than a mere mental exercise. It is the cultivation of a mindset that seeks to understand and live in harmony with the truths revealed in the Bible.

The importance of this alignment cannot be overstated. Proverbs 4:23 (ASV) warns us, "Keep thy heart with all diligence; For out of it are the issues of life." Our thoughts shape our attitudes, actions, and ultimately, our lives. If our thoughts are in sync with God's truth, our lives will reflect His wisdom and goodness.

So, what are the impacts of aligning our thoughts with God's truth?

1. Empowerment to Overcome Sin: When we imbibe God's truth, we are empowered to overcome sin. Hebrews 4:12 (ESV) describes the Word of God as "living and active, sharper than any two-edged sword, piercing to the division of soul and of spirit, of joints and of marrow, and discerning the thoughts and intentions of the heart." By aligning our thoughts with this powerful Word, we can discern and resist sinful tendencies.

2. Living in Freedom: Aligning our thoughts with God's truth sets us free from the bondages of guilt, fear, and condemnation. Jesus assures in John 8:32 (ESV), "And you will know the truth, and the truth will set you free." When we replace lies with God's truth, we experience the freedom Christ offers.

3. Enjoying Peace: God's truth brings peace. In the midst of life's storms, remembering God's promises and faithfulness brings tranquility to our hearts. As Paul urges in Philippians 4:8 (ESV), "Finally, brothers, whatever is true, whatever is honorable, whatever is just, whatever is pure, whatever is lovely, whatever is commendable, if there is any excellence, if there is anything worthy of praise, think about these things."

4. Bearing Fruit: When our thoughts are aligned with God's truth, we bear spiritual fruit. Jesus stated in John 15:4-5 (ESV), "Abide in me, and I in you. As the branch cannot bear fruit by itself, unless it abides in the vine, neither can you, unless you abide in me... for apart from me you can do nothing." Abiding in Christ involves abiding in His Word, His truth. Doing so produces spiritual fruit in our lives.

5. Experiencing True Joy: Knowing and living in God's truth brings joy. David writes in Psalm 16:11 (ASV), "Thou wilt show me the path of life: In thy presence is fullness of joy; In thy right hand there are pleasures for evermore." The joy derived from aligning our thoughts with God's truth surpasses worldly pleasures and is everlasting.

In summary, aligning our thoughts with God's truth is a crucial part of renewing our minds and breaking free from negative patterns. As our minds are filled with God's truth, we become more like Christ and can impact the world in a significant way. This alignment is a transformative process that results in a life of victory, peace, fruitfulness, and joy—a life that truly makes a difference.

Challenging Negative Thoughts and Beliefs

Learning Strategies to Challenge and Replace Negative Thoughts

The journey to breaking free from negative patterns involves learning to challenge and replace negative thoughts with the truth of God's Word. Here are practical strategies, drawn from Scripture, to assist in this transformative process:

1. Identify the Negative Thoughts: The first step in challenging negative thoughts is to identify them. As stated in Hebrews 4:12 (ESV), the Word of God is "discerning the thoughts and intentions of the heart." Spending time in God's Word helps us to recognize thoughts that are not aligned with His truth.

2. Challenge Negative Thoughts with Scripture: Once we identify a negative thought, we should challenge it with Scripture. Jesus models this in Matthew 4:1-11 (ESV) when He was tempted by the devil in the wilderness. Each time the devil tempted Him, Jesus responded by quoting Scripture. We too can use Scripture to challenge negative thoughts.

3. Replace Negative Thoughts with God's Truth: It is not enough to challenge negative thoughts; we must replace them with God's truth. Paul instructs in Philippians 4:8 (ESV), "Finally, brothers, whatever is true, whatever is honorable, whatever is just, whatever is pure, whatever is lovely, whatever is commendable, if there is any excellence, if there is anything worthy of praise, think about these things."

4. Memorize Scripture: Memorizing Scripture enables us to have God's Word readily available to counter negative thoughts. Psalm 119:11 (ASV) says, "Thy word have I laid up in my heart, That I might not sin against thee."

5. Pray for Renewal of Mind: Prayer is a powerful tool in the process of mind renewal. Paul advises in Romans 12:2 (ESV), "Do not be conformed to this world, but be transformed by the renewal of your mind, that by testing you may discern what is the will of God, what is good and acceptable and perfect." As we pray, God works in us to renew our minds and align our thoughts with His.

6. Cultivate Godly Fellowship: The company we keep influences our thought patterns. Proverbs 13:20 (ASV) reminds us, "Walk with the wise, and thou shalt be wise." Cultivating relationships with godly individuals can aid in challenging and replacing negative thoughts.

7. Meditate on God's Word: Lastly, meditating on God's Word helps us focus on His truth and replaces negative thought patterns. Psalm 1:2 (ESV) describes the person who meditates on God's law day and night as blessed and fruitful.

In summary, breaking free from negative patterns involves a conscious effort to identify, challenge, and replace negative thoughts with the truth of God's Word. Through the diligent study of Scripture, prayer, godly fellowship, and meditation on God's Word, we can align our thoughts with God's truth and experience the transformative power of renewing our minds in Christ.

Embracing the Truth of God's Word to Counteract Negative Beliefs

In the battle against negative thought patterns and beliefs, the truth of God's Word is our strongest weapon. We can embrace God's truth not as mere suggestions or philosophical ideals, but as the authoritative and infallible standard against which all thoughts and beliefs should be measured. Here are key strategies to embrace the truth of God's Word and counteract negative beliefs:

1. Understand the Authority of God's Word: The Bible, as the inspired, inerrant Word of God, carries ultimate authority over our thoughts and beliefs. 2 Timothy 3:16-17 (ESV) states, "All Scripture is breathed out by God and profitable for teaching, for reproof, for correction, and for training in righteousness, that the man of God may be complete, equipped for every good work."

2. Believe in the Power of God's Word: God's Word is not just informative, but transformative. As Hebrews 4:12 (ASV) states, "For the word of God is living, and active, and sharper than any two-edged sword." It possesses the power to reach into our thoughts and intentions, challenging and changing our deep-seated beliefs.

3. Daily Intake of God's Word: To counteract negative beliefs, we need a daily intake of God's truth. Psalm 1:2 (ESV) praises the one "whose delight is in the law of the LORD, and on his law he meditates day and night."

4. Pray for Understanding: Embracing God's truth involves praying for understanding. In Psalm 119:34 (ASV), the psalmist asks God, "Give me understanding, and I shall keep thy law; Yea, I shall observe it with my whole heart."

5. Apply God's Word: Merely reading or hearing God's Word is insufficient; we must apply it to our lives. James 1:22 (ESV) urges us to be "doers of the word, and not hearers only, deceiving yourselves."

6. Share God's Word with Others: Sharing God's Word with others helps us internalize His truths and counteract negative beliefs. As we articulate God's truth, it further cements these truths in our minds and hearts.

7. Allow the Holy Spirit to Guide You: As believers, we are not alone in our struggle against negative beliefs. The Holy Spirit, who dwells within us, guides us into all truth (John 16:13, ESV).

In summary, embracing the truth of God's Word to counteract negative beliefs involves recognizing the authority and power of Scripture, engaging in daily intake of the Word, praying for understanding, applying the Word, sharing the Word with others, and depending on the Holy Spirit. When we embrace God's truth wholeheartedly, we find that His Word is indeed "a lamp to our feet and a light to our path" (Psalm 119:105, ASV), guiding us away from negative beliefs and towards His truth and life.

Embracing the Truth of Your Identity in Christ

Discovering Your True Identity as a Child of God

One of the most transformative steps in breaking free from negative patterns and renewing our minds in Christ is discovering our true identity as children of God. This concept is not just a religious phrase, but a profound truth that can revolutionize our lives and perspectives.

1. A Child of God Through Faith in Jesus Christ: Galatians 3:26 (ESV) states, "For in Christ Jesus you are all sons of God, through faith." By placing our faith in Jesus Christ, we are adopted into God's family. This adoption grants us a new identity - we are no longer slaves to sin, but children of God.

2. A New Creation: The moment we accept Christ, we become a new creation. As it is written in 2 Corinthians 5:17 (ASV), "Therefore if any man is in Christ, he is a new creature: the old things are passed away; behold, they are become new." This new identity eradicates the old negative patterns and equips us with a fresh start.

3. God's Chosen People: In 1 Peter 2:9 (ESV), the Bible says, "But you are a chosen race, a royal priesthood, a holy nation, a people for his own possession, that you may proclaim the excellencies of him who called you out of darkness into his marvelous light." As children of God, we are chosen, royal, holy, and treasured.

4. A Temple of the Holy Spirit: Our bodies are the temple of the Holy Spirit. This truth, emphasized in 1 Corinthians 6:19 (ASV), underscores the immense value and dignity we carry as God's children. It also serves as a deterrent against negative behaviors and thoughts, reminding us of the sacred presence within us.

5. An Heir of God: As a child of God, we are heirs of God and co-heirs with Christ, as indicated in Romans 8:17 (ESV). We have an eternal inheritance that can never perish, spoil, or fade.

6. God's Workmanship: Ephesians 2:10 (ASV) declares that we are God's workmanship, created in Christ Jesus for good works. This aspect of our identity fuels our purpose and mission in life, prompting us to live for something greater than ourselves.

Discovering your true identity as a child of God is a transformative experience. It not only reshapes your self-perception but also influences your actions, decisions, and life purpose. Knowing you are a child of God, a new creation, chosen, a temple of the Holy Spirit, an heir of God, and God's workmanship will empower you to break free from negative patterns and live a life centered in Christ. Recognize this truth, meditate on it, and allow it to renew your mind daily. This understanding is key to making a difference in your life and in the lives of those around you.

Letting Go of False Labels and Embracing Your Identity in Christ

Life experiences and societal pressures can often lead us to adopt labels that are not reflective of our true identity as children of God. These false labels can create negative patterns and hinder our ability to live in the fullness of who we are in Christ. The process of renewing our minds involves acknowledging these false labels, releasing them, and replacing them with the truth of God's Word.

1. Identifying False Labels: False labels can take many forms, such as "unworthy," "failure," "rejected," or "unlovable." These labels often stem from past hurts, rejections, failures, or negative messages received from others. It's important to identify these false labels and understand their source.

2. The Danger of False Labels: False labels can be harmful because they distort our perception of ourselves and of God. They can create feelings of shame, fear, insecurity, and defeat. More so, they can prevent us from living out our true identity and purpose in Christ (Proverbs 23:7 ASV, "For as he thinketh within himself, so is he").

3. Releasing False Labels: To release false labels, we must confront them with the truth of God's Word. As Hebrews 4:12 (ESV) says, "For the word of God is living and active, sharper than any two-edged sword, piercing to the division of soul and of spirit, of joints and of marrow, and discerning the thoughts and intentions of the heart." God's Word can reveal and sever the lies that we've believed about ourselves.

4. Embracing Your Identity in Christ: When we let go of false labels, we can fully embrace our identity in Christ. This identity is rooted in God's unchanging truth and not in our feelings, achievements, failures, or the opinions of others. It includes being God's child (John 1:12 ESV), a friend of Jesus (John 15:15 ASV), justified and redeemed (Romans 3:24 ESV), and a temple of the Holy Spirit (1 Corinthians 6:19 ASV).

5. Affirming Your Identity in Christ: The process of embracing our identity in Christ also involves regular affirmation. Speak out biblical truths about your identity and replace the old, false labels with God's truths. For instance, instead of agreeing with the label "unlovable," affirm what the Bible says in Romans 5:8 (ESV), "But God shows his love for us in that while we were still sinners, Christ died for us."

6. Living Out Your Identity in Christ: Finally, living out our identity in Christ involves aligning our thoughts, words, and actions with God's truth. As we believe and live according to our true identity, we will experience freedom, joy, and fulfillment in Christ.

Letting go of false labels and embracing our identity in Christ is a vital step in breaking free from negative patterns. It requires courage, honesty, and reliance on God's Word. As we allow the truth of who we are in Christ to renew our minds, we become empowered to make a difference in our lives and the lives of those around us.

Practicing Self-Reflection and Prayer

Cultivating a Habit of Self-Reflection and Examining Your Thought Patterns

The journey towards renewing the mind in Christ is paved with consistent self-reflection and examination of one's thought patterns. It is an intentional process that allows us to align our thoughts with God's truth, ultimately enabling us to break free from negative patterns that can inhibit our spiritual growth and effectiveness.

1. The Need for Self-Reflection: In a world inundated with distractions and busyness, cultivating a habit of self-reflection is vital. It allows us to pause, evaluate our thoughts, feelings, and actions, and align them with God's Word. Psalm 139:23-24 (ASV) speaks to this need: "Search me, O God, and know my heart: Try me, and know my thoughts; And see if there be any wicked way in me, And lead me in the way everlasting."

2. How to Self-Reflect: Self-reflection is a practice that can be done in several ways. It could involve setting aside a specific time each day to ponder your thoughts and actions, journaling about your experiences and observations, or even engaging in silent meditation and prayer, inviting the Holy Spirit to illuminate areas in your life that need change.

3. Examining Your Thought Patterns: This aspect of self-reflection involves observing the recurring thoughts that dominate your mind. These patterns of thought can significantly influence your behaviors and emotions. Romans 12:2 (ESV) tells us, "Do not be conformed to this world, but be transformed by the renewal of your mind, that by testing you may discern what is the will of God, what is good and acceptable and perfect."

4. The Danger of Negative Thought Patterns: Negative thought patterns, often manifesting as fears, doubts, guilt, or self-deprecation, can impede our relationship with God and hinder us from living out our identity in Christ. They can also affect our emotional health and relationships with others.

5. Applying God's Word in Self-Reflection: The Word of God is the ultimate standard by which we should measure our thoughts and actions. Hebrews 4:12 (ESV) provides a vivid description of its power: "For the word of God is living and active, sharper than any two-edged sword, piercing to the division of soul and of spirit, of joints and of marrow, and discerning the thoughts and intentions of the heart."

6. Cultivating Positive Thought Patterns: As we evaluate our thoughts through the lens of Scripture, we can begin to replace negative thought patterns with positive, biblical ones. Philippians 4:8 (ASV) encourages us to think about things that are true, honorable, just, pure, lovely, and of good report.

Cultivating a habit of self-reflection and examining our thought patterns is crucial for renewing our minds in Christ. As we make it a practice to hold our thoughts against the truth of God's Word, we will be better equipped to break free from negative patterns, live according to our true identity in Christ, and make a meaningful difference in our spheres of influence.

Engaging in Prayer as a Means of Surrendering Negative Patterns to God

As we strive to break free from negative patterns and renew our minds in Christ, prayer becomes an essential practice in our lives.

Prayer is not merely a religious duty or ritual; it is a personal communion with God that allows us to surrender our thoughts, attitudes, and actions to His will and power.

1. The Power of Prayer: Prayer has a transformative power that is beyond human understanding. It is the channel through which God's divine power flows into our lives, bringing about change and renewal. James 5:16 (ESV) affirms, "The prayer of a righteous person has great power as it is working."

2. Prayer as Surrender: Engaging in prayer is an act of surrender. It is a confession that we are not self-sufficient and that we need God's guidance, strength, and wisdom to overcome our negative thought patterns. As we pray, we acknowledge our weaknesses and invite God to transform us by His strength.

3. How to Surrender Negative Patterns in Prayer: When you engage in prayer, bring your thoughts before God honestly and openly. Admit your struggles, confess your sins, and express your desire to have your mind renewed in Christ. Psalm 51:10 (ASV), a prayer of King David after his sin with Bathsheba, can serve as a model: "Create in me a clean heart, O God; And renew a right spirit within me."

4. God's Response to Our Prayers: God hears our prayers and responds with love, grace, and power. He does not promise to remove all our struggles immediately, but He guarantees to provide us with the strength and wisdom we need to overcome them. In 2 Corinthians 12:9 (ESV), the Apostle Paul recounts God's response to his plea for relief from a persistent problem, "But he said to me, 'My grace is sufficient for you, for my power is made perfect in weakness.'"

5. Persistence in Prayer: The process of breaking free from negative patterns and renewing our minds in Christ is often gradual and requires perseverance. In Luke 18:1 (ESV), Jesus taught His disciples that "they ought always to pray and not lose heart." This admonition serves as a reminder for us to persist in prayer, especially when we are dealing with deep-seated negative patterns.

6. The Role of God's Word in Prayer: As we engage in prayer, it is beneficial to incorporate God's Word. Scripture not only provides a guide for our prayers but also aligns our desires with God's will. By praying according to God's Word, we are effectively surrendering our thoughts to His truth.

Engaging in prayer as a means of surrendering negative patterns to God is a transformative practice that every Christian should embrace. It involves admitting our weaknesses, surrendering our control, seeking God's will, and trusting in His power to change us. It is through this practice of prayerful surrender that we can experience the renewal of our minds and lives in Christ.

Surrounding Yourself with Positive Influences

Building a Supportive Community of Believers Who Encourage Growth and Transformation

Community is at the heart of Christian faith and growth. Just as a coal glows in the fire but dims when isolated, so does a believer's faith grow stronger in the company of others. In a supportive community of believers, Christians find the environment they need to challenge negative patterns and renew their minds in Christ.

1. The Biblical Mandate for Christian Community: The Bible underscores the importance of fellowship among believers. In Hebrews 10:24-25 (ESV), we are encouraged to consider "how to stir up one another to love and good works, not neglecting to meet together, as is the habit of some, but encouraging one another, and all the more as you see the Day drawing near."

2. Encouraging One Another Towards Growth and Transformation: In a Christian community, believers have a responsibility to build up each other in faith, hope, and love. The Apostle Paul emphasizes this in 1 Thessalonians 5:11 (ESV): "Therefore encourage one another and build one another up, just as you are doing." Encouragement isn't merely offering comforting words; it's about inspiring others towards spiritual growth and transformation.

3. The Role of Accountability: A supportive community promotes accountability, which is crucial for breaking free from negative patterns. When we know others are aware of our struggle, it motivates us to stay committed to change. Proverbs 27:17 (ASV) says, "Iron sharpens iron; so a man sharpeneth the countenance of his friend." This mutual sharpening leads to personal and spiritual growth.

4. Practicing Confession and Forgiveness: In James 5:16 (ESV), we read, "Therefore, confess your sins to one another and pray for one another, that you may be healed." A community grounded in Christ practices confession and forgiveness, providing a safe environment for individuals to overcome negative patterns.

5. The Necessity of Diverse Gifts: The Apostle Paul describes the church as a body with many parts, each with different functions (1 Corinthians 12:12-27, ESV). This diversity of gifts contributes to the overall health and growth of the community, enabling individuals to address different areas of their life that need transformation.

6. The Role of Leadership: Sound, Biblically-based leadership is crucial in fostering a supportive community. Leaders are to equip the saints for the work of ministry and the building up of the body of Christ (Ephesians 4:11-13, ESV).

Building a supportive community of believers is not a mere suggestion, but a Biblical command. It offers the setting necessary for believers to grow in their faith, challenge negative patterns, and experience renewal in Christ. By encouraging one another, holding each other accountable, practicing confession and forgiveness, appreciating diverse gifts, and fostering good leadership, we can create a community that enables every believer to make a difference.

Seeking Mentorship and Accountability to Help Break Free from Negative Patterns

Mentorship and accountability play pivotal roles in breaking free from negative patterns and renewing the mind in Christ. These twin pillars foster an environment conducive to spiritual growth and transformation, aiding believers in their pursuit of a Christ-centered life.

1. The Role of Mentorship in Spiritual Growth: Mentorship in the Christian context is a relational experience through which one person empowers another by sharing God-given resources. Timothy's relationship with Paul in the New Testament exemplifies this. In 2 Timothy 1:13 (ESV), Paul advises Timothy, "Follow the pattern of the sound words that you have heard from me, in the faith and love that are in Christ Jesus."

2. The Importance of Selecting a Mentor: The choice of a mentor should not be taken lightly. A good mentor will have a vibrant, evident relationship with Christ, a lifestyle that aligns with biblical principles, and the wisdom to provide spiritual guidance (Titus 2:3-5, ESV).

3. The Role of Accountability in Breaking Negative Patterns: Accountability is the willingness to open our lives to a few carefully selected, trusted, loyal confidants who speak the truth—who have the right to examine, to question, to appraise, and to give counsel. Proverbs 27:17 (ASV) points out, "Iron sharpeneth iron; So a man sharpeneth the countenance of his friend."

4. Fostering an Accountability Relationship: An accountability relationship should be marked by trust, respect, and mutual spiritual growth. James 5:16 (ESV) instructs, "Therefore, confess your sins to one another and pray for one another, that you may be healed." This verse illustrates the essence of accountability, highlighting the need for confession, prayer, and spiritual healing.

5. Balancing Mentorship and Accountability: A healthy Christian walk benefits from both mentorship and accountability. While a mentor provides guidance and imparts wisdom, an accountability partner ensures we stay on the right path, challenging us to break free from negative patterns and live in alignment with Christ.

6. Living a Transformed Life: A transformed life is the ultimate testament to successful mentorship and accountability. Romans 12:2 (ESV) says, "Do not be conformed to this world, but be transformed by the renewal of your mind, that by testing you may discern what is the will of God, what is good and acceptable and perfect."

In conclusion, seeking mentorship and accountability is a crucial step in renewing our minds in Christ. As we submit ourselves to the godly influence of mentors and the watchful care of accountability partners, we find the strength and wisdom to break free from negative patterns and live out our true identity in Christ.

Walking in Freedom and Transformation

Applying Biblical Principles to Experience Lasting Change and Transformation

The process of breaking free from negative patterns involves more than simply acknowledging the existence of these patterns. It requires an intentional commitment to apply biblical principles, leading to lasting change and transformation.

1. The Principle of Renewal of the Mind: At the core of lasting change is the renewal of the mind. As stated in Romans 12:2 (ESV), "Do not be conformed to this world, but be transformed by the renewal of your mind, that by testing you may discern what is the will of God, what is good and acceptable and perfect." This verse highlights the need for cognitive transformation as a prerequisite for discerning God's will and achieving spiritual growth.

2. The Principle of Reconciliation with God: Experiencing transformation requires that we reconcile ourselves with God, accepting His forgiveness, and learning to live in the light of His grace. Colossians 1:21-22 (ESV) affirms, "And you, who once were alienated and hostile in mind, doing evil deeds, he has now reconciled in his body of flesh by his death, in order to present you holy and blameless and above reproach before him."

3. The Principle of Living by Faith: Living by faith and not by sight is a crucial principle in experiencing God's transformation. It is faith that helps us to see beyond our present circumstances and fosters hope in the promises of God. 2 Corinthians 5:7 (ASV) succinctly puts it: "For we walk by faith, not by sight."

4. The Principle of Godly Obedience: True transformation is demonstrated through obedience to God's commands. The psalmist in Psalm 119:11 (ESV) states, "I have stored up your word in my heart, that I might not sin against you." This signifies a proactive stance in applying God's Word to one's life as a means of avoiding sin.

5. The Principle of Christlikeness: The ultimate goal of transformation is to become more like Christ. The Apostle Paul writes in Philippians 2:5 (ESV), "Have this mind among yourselves, which is yours in Christ Jesus," suggesting that we should adopt the same humble, selfless mindset that Christ exhibited during His time on earth.

6. The Principle of Perseverance: The process of transformation is ongoing and requires perseverance. Galatians 6:9 (ESV) encourages, "And let us not grow weary of doing good, for in due season we will reap, if we do not give up." This passage illustrates the need for persistence in the face of adversity.

In conclusion, experiencing lasting change and transformation is contingent on applying these biblical principles. This process calls for the renewal of the mind, reconciliation with God, living by faith, obedience to God's Word, striving for Christlikeness, and a perseverance that does not waver. By embodying these principles, we pave the way for the Holy Spirit to bring about deep, lasting change in our lives, helping us break free from negative patterns.

Embracing the Abundant Life God Has Planned for You, Free from Negative Patterns

The culmination of breaking free from negative patterns is the joyful embrace of the abundant life God has planned for us. This does not mean a life free of challenges or hardships, but rather, a life where we are not held captive by these patterns and are free to live according to God's will and plan.

In John 10:10 (ESV), Jesus said, "The thief comes only to steal and kill and destroy. I came that they may have life and have it abundantly." Here, Jesus emphasizes His purpose for coming to earth, to provide a life characterized by overflowing fullness and richness - an abundant life. But what does this abundant life look like?

1. A Life Marked by Peace: With the negative patterns and sinful habits behind, we begin to experience the "peace of God, which surpasses all understanding" (Philippians 4:7, ESV). This peace, rooted in our restored relationship with God, is not contingent on external circumstances, but is a pervasive tranquility that stems from knowing God is in control.

2. A Life Filled with Joy: True joy, as a fruit of the Spirit (Galatians 5:22, ESV), becomes a part of our character. Even in the face of adversity, we have an internal sense of happiness and contentment because we know God is working all things together for our good (Romans 8:28, ESV).

3. A Life Driven by Purpose: Free from the shackles of negative patterns, we can fully engage in the purpose for which we were created. As it says in Ephesians 2:10 (ESV), "For we are his workmanship, created in Christ Jesus for good works, which God prepared beforehand, that we should walk in them."

4. A Life of Freedom: Galatians 5:1 (ESV) declares, "For freedom Christ has set us free; stand firm therefore, and do not submit again to a yoke of slavery." Liberated from negative patterns, we are free to live in the light of God's grace, not constrained by the limitations of our old nature.

5. A Life of Love: Being released from negative patterns allows us to experience and manifest God's love more deeply. As it says in Romans 13:10 (ESV), "Love does no wrong to a neighbor; therefore love is the fulfilling of the law."

6. A Life of Service: When we are not dominated by negative patterns, we are free to serve God and others. Jesus, in Mark 10:45 (ESV), asserted, "For even the Son of Man came not to be served but to serve, and to give his life as a ransom for many."

Embracing the abundant life that God has planned for us requires conscious effort and active participation on our part. It demands that we surrender daily to God, seek His will in all things, and strive to live a life worthy of the calling we have received (Ephesians 4:1, ESV). In doing so, we open ourselves to the richness and fullness of life that God has always intended for us, a life truly free from the bondage of negative patterns.

APPENDIX B Discovering Your Identity in Christ: Embracing Your True Worth

Understanding Your Identity in Christ

Recognizing Your True Worth as a Child of God

Recognizing our true worth as a child of God is an essential step in discovering our identity in Christ. In the world's eyes, our worth may be tied to external factors like wealth, success, beauty, or power. Yet, in God's sight, our value is intrinsically connected to our identity as His beloved children.

You Are Created in God's Image

Genesis 1:27 (ASV) states, "And God created man in his own image, in the image of God created he him; male and female created he them." This foundational truth reveals that we carry within us the imprint of the divine. Being made in God's image means we reflect His character, creativity, capacity for relationship, and moral responsibility. This intrinsic worth does not fluctuate based on our performance, successes, or failures.

You Are Loved Unconditionally

One of the most profound truths that highlight our worth is the unchanging, unfathomable love that God has for us. Romans 5:8 (ESV) attests, "But God shows his love for us in that while we were still sinners, Christ died for us." God's love was so great that He gave His only Son to redeem us, even when we were lost in sin. This extraordinary act of love demonstrates our tremendous value in His eyes.

You Are Redeemed and Forgiven

Our worth is also underscored by our redemption through Jesus Christ. Ephesians 1:7 (ESV) proclaims, "In him we have redemption through his blood, the forgiveness of our trespasses, according to the riches of his grace." As forgiven and redeemed people, we are no longer defined by our past mistakes but by God's grace and mercy.

You Are a New Creation

The transformation that occurs when we accept Christ is another testament to our worth. 2 Corinthians 5:17 (ESV) declares, "Therefore, if anyone is in Christ, he is a new creation. The old has passed away; behold, the new has come." As new creations, we are no longer bound by our old identities. Our value is now defined by our new identity in Christ, set free from the power of sin and equipped to live a life that honors God.

You Are Co-Heirs with Christ

Romans 8:17 (ESV) affirms, "And if children, then heirs—heirs of God and fellow heirs with Christ, provided we suffer with him in order that we may also be glorified with him." As children of God, we are entitled to an inheritance that includes all the spiritual blessings of the Kingdom. This royal standing underscores our immense worth as God's children.

You Are God's Workmanship

Ephesians 2:10 (ESV) states, "For we are his workmanship, created in Christ Jesus for good works, which God prepared beforehand, that we should walk in them." As His workmanship, or masterpiece, we are uniquely designed by the Master Artist for a specific purpose. This not only signifies our intrinsic worth but also emphasizes our divine calling.

Recognizing our true worth as children of God liberates us from the need for external validation. It instills in us a profound sense of security, purpose, and identity rooted in Christ. In this realization, we are freed to live out our God-given potential and to embrace fully the abundant life He offers us. Remember, your worth does not lie in worldly measures but in the unchanging truth of God's love for you. You are His precious child, and nothing can ever diminish that value.

Embracing the Love and Acceptance Found in Christ

Unconditional love and acceptance are fundamental human needs. We thrive when we know we are loved just as we are, without conditions. While the world often conditions love and acceptance on performance, looks, or status, Christ offers us a love that is unconditional and acceptance that is unequivocal. Embracing the love and acceptance found in Christ leads to profound personal transformation and fulfillment.

Experiencing God's Unconditional Love

The love of God is not like human love. It does not fluctuate based on our behavior, performance, or change in circumstances. Romans 8:38-39 (ESV) assures us, "For I am sure that neither death nor life, nor angels nor rulers, nor things present nor things to come, nor powers, nor height nor depth, nor anything else in all creation, will be able to separate us from the love of God in Christ Jesus our Lord." This means that nothing we do, no mistake or failure, can separate us from God's love.

This understanding changes everything. When we recognize that we are loved beyond measure, just as we are, it brings a profound sense of peace, security, and well-being. It empowers us to live freely and authentically, unafraid of rejection or condemnation.

Finding Complete Acceptance in Christ

In addition to unconditional love, Christ offers us complete acceptance. In the eyes of the world, we often fall short. We are not perfect, and we bear the scars of past mistakes. But God, in His boundless grace, accepts us just as we are. Ephesians 1:6 (ESV) declares, "to the praise of his glorious grace, with which he has blessed us in the Beloved."

In Christ, we are not only accepted but also cherished and valued. This acceptance is not dependent on our ability to earn it but is a free gift from a loving God. It doesn't mean God overlooks our sin. Instead, He fully acknowledges our fallen nature, yet He loves us so much that He made a way through Christ for us to be accepted in spite of our shortcomings.

Living in the Light of Love and Acceptance

Embracing God's love and acceptance impacts every area of our lives. It frees us from the tyranny of people's opinions and the crippling fear of rejection. We no longer have to strive for acceptance or prove our worth. Our value is secure in Christ, and our identity is firmly rooted in His love for us. This security enables us to live boldly and confidently, knowing that we are deeply loved and fully accepted by our Heavenly Father.

Cherishing Our Identity in Christ

When we grasp the depth of God's love and acceptance, we start to see ourselves differently. We are no longer defined by our past, our failures, or our inadequacies. Instead, we are defined by Christ and His work in us. Galatians 2:20 (ESV) articulates this beautifully: "I have been crucified with Christ. It is no longer I who live, but Christ who lives in me. And the life I now live in the flesh I live by faith in the Son of God, who loved me and gave himself for me."

Understanding and accepting our identity in Christ is fundamental to our spiritual growth and overall well-being. Embracing God's love and acceptance leads to transformation, freedom, and a deep sense of joy and fulfillment. It is the first step towards living the abundant life that Christ promised and making a difference in the world around us.

Embracing God's Unchanging Word

The Authority and Reliability of the Bible in Shaping Our Identity

The Bible, as the inspired, inerrant Word of God, carries ultimate authority in our lives. The Scripture is not just a historical document or a compilation of moral teachings. It is a divine revelation that speaks truth into our lives and shapes our identity. As 2 Timothy 3:16 (ESV) asserts, "All Scripture is breathed out by God and profitable for teaching, for reproof, for correction, and for training in righteousness."

The Bible as the Inspired Word of God

The Bible's authority derives from its divine origin. As you noted, the Bible is inspired, implying that its authors were moved along by the Holy Spirit. This divine inspiration ensures that the Bible's content is not merely human words or ideas, but God's own words and thoughts. It also ensures the Bible's inerrancy and infallibility, making it a trustworthy and reliable guide for life.

The Authority of the Bible in Defining Our Identity

The Bible does more than convey historical events or theological concepts. It reveals God's character, His purposes, and His plans for humanity. Through the Bible, we learn who we are in relation to God.

When we seek to define our identity, we must turn to the Bible as our ultimate authority. It tells us that we are created in God's image (Genesis 1:27, ASV), redeemed by Christ (Ephesians 1:7, ESV), and sanctified by the Spirit (1 Corinthians 6:11, ESV). This biblical understanding of our identity supersedes all other labels or identities the world may try to impose on us.

The Reliability of the Bible in Shaping Our Identity

The Bible's reliability is rooted in its inerrancy and infallibility. If we believe in the inspiration of Scripture, we must also trust in its reliability. This means that we can depend on its teachings to accurately shape our understanding of ourselves and our role in God's story.

Many passages affirm the reliability of the Bible. Psalm 119:160 (ASV) declares, "The sum of thy word is truth; And every one of thy righteous ordinances endureth forever." Furthermore, Jesus Himself affirmed the enduring nature of God's Word when He said, "Heaven and earth will pass away, but my words will not pass away" (Matthew 24:35, ESV).

Living in Light of the Bible's Authority and Reliability

Understanding the authority and reliability of the Bible is one thing, but living in light of this understanding is another. It requires that we study the Bible diligently, meditate on its truths, and apply its teachings to our lives. This is how we allow the Word of God to shape our identity and guide our actions.

Moreover, we must defend the Bible's authority and reliability in a world that often rejects absolute truth. As Peter instructed in 1 Peter 3:15 (ESV), "but in your hearts honor Christ the Lord as holy, always being prepared to make a defense to anyone who asks you for a reason for the hope that is in you; yet do it with gentleness and respect."

Our identity in Christ, as revealed through the authoritative and reliable Scripture, is the foundation of our Christian life. It influences how we perceive ourselves, how we relate to God and others, and how we engage with the world. As we embrace this identity, we will indeed make a difference, demonstrating the transformative power of the Gospel in our lives.

Studying Scripture to Discover Our True Identity in Christ

The Bible isn't just a book; it's a mirror that reflects who we are and who we are meant to be. When we read and study Scripture with an open heart, we begin to see our true selves—our weaknesses and flaws, but more importantly, our true identity in Christ. As James 1:23-25 (ESV) says, "For if anyone is a hearer of the word and not a doer, he is like a man who looks intently at his natural face in a mirror... But the one who looks into the perfect law, the law of liberty, and perseveres, being no hearer who forgets but a doer who acts, he will be blessed in his doing."

Understanding Who We Are: Created, Fallen, and Redeemed

The Bible provides us with a comprehensive understanding of our identity. It reveals that we are created by God in His image (Genesis 1:27, ASV), implying that we are intrinsically valuable and capable of reflecting God's character.

However, the Bible also narrates how humanity fell into sin, resulting in a broken relationship with God (Genesis 3, ASV). We are fallen beings, tainted by sin, and inclined towards rebellion.

Yet, this is not the end of our story. The Bible proclaims the good news of our redemption in Christ. Jesus' death and resurrection reconcile us with God, making us a new creation (2 Corinthians 5:17, ESV). Therefore, our true identity is that we are beloved children of God, redeemed and restored through Christ's sacrifice.

Studying Scripture to Discover Our Identity in Christ

Studying the Bible is integral to understanding our identity in Christ. We do not study Scripture merely to increase our knowledge, but to transform our hearts and minds.

1. **Regular Bible Reading**: Consistent interaction with God's Word is critical. Through regular reading, we familiarize ourselves with the grand narrative of Scripture and learn the character of God and our place in His story.
2. **Meditation and Reflection**: As we read, we must also meditate on God's Word and reflect on its implications for our lives. This involves considering how the truths we read affect our understanding of who we are in Christ.
3. **Application**: James 1:22 (ESV) warns, "But be doers of the word, and not hearers only, deceiving yourselves." It is not enough to merely read and understand Scripture. We must also apply it to our lives. When Scripture reveals aspects of our identity in Christ, we must strive to live in a manner that aligns with this identity.
4. **Prayerful Study**: Prayer is an essential part of Bible study. As we read and study Scripture, we should regularly pause to pray, asking God to open our minds and hearts to understand His Word and reveal our identity in Christ.

The Impact of Discovering Our Identity in Christ

Discovering our true identity in Christ transforms our lives. It changes our perspective on self, God, and others. We learn to see ourselves not through the lens of our past failures or the world's expectations, but through Christ's redeeming work.

Our identity in Christ also affects how we relate to God. Understanding that we are beloved children of God deepens our relationship with Him. It assures us of His love and care and motivates us to live in obedience to Him.

Furthermore, our identity in Christ changes how we relate to others. Knowing that we are loved and accepted in Christ empowers us to extend the same love and acceptance to others.

Indeed, studying Scripture to discover our true identity in Christ is not just a personal pursuit; it has profound implications for our relationships and our engagement with the world. As we grow in our understanding of our identity in Christ, we will truly make a difference in our world, reflecting the love and grace of Christ in all we do.

Renewing Your Mind

Overcoming Negative Thoughts and Lies with God's Truth

The battleground of our identities often takes place in our minds. Negative thoughts, self-doubt, and lies from the enemy can cloud our understanding of who we truly are. Yet, God's truth is a powerful weapon to combat these falsehoods. "The weapons we fight with are not the weapons of the world. On the contrary, they have divine power to demolish strongholds. We demolish arguments and every pretension that sets itself up against the knowledge of God, and we take captive every thought to make it obedient to Christ" (2 Corinthians 10:4-5, ESV).

Recognizing the Lies

The first step to overcoming these negative thoughts is recognizing the lies we've been believing. Satan, the father of lies (John 8:44, ESV), seeks to deceive us into believing falsehoods about ourselves and our identities in Christ. These lies often revolve around our worth, our abilities, our past failures, or our future potential.

Confronting Lies with Truth

The second step is confronting these lies with God's truth. Every lie we believe has a counter truth in God's Word. We must diligently study the Scriptures and arm ourselves with God's truths about our identity in Christ.

Remember, God's Word affirms that we are loved (Romans 5:8, ESV), chosen (Ephesians 1:4, ESV), forgiven (1 John 1:9, ESV), and created for a purpose (Ephesians 2:10, ESV). These truths are our defense against the enemy's lies.

Replacing Lies with God's Truth

The third step involves replacing the lies we've believed with the truth of God's Word. This process involves actively rejecting the lie and affirming the corresponding truth from Scripture. For example, if we're struggling with the lie that we're unlovable because of our past, we should remind ourselves of Romans 5:8 (ESV): "But God shows his love for us in that while we were still sinners, Christ died for us."

Renewing Our Minds in Christ

The Apostle Paul urged believers in Romans 12:2 (ESV): "Do not be conformed to this world, but be transformed by the renewal of your mind, that by testing you may discern what is the will of God, what is good and acceptable and perfect." Renewing our minds involves allowing God's truth to reshape our thought patterns, perceptions, and beliefs about ourselves. It's a process of transformation from the inside out that affects our feelings, decisions, and actions.

The Power of God's Word

God's Word is a lamp unto our feet and a light unto our path (Psalms 119:105, ASV). It illuminates our minds, giving us insight into who we are and how we are to live. By studying Scripture, we discover our true worth and identity in Christ.

As we replace the lies and negative thoughts we've held onto with God's truth, we'll experience a profound transformation in our lives. This process isn't a one-time event; it's a lifelong journey. Yet, as we continue in this journey, we'll grow more into the image of Christ, reflecting His love and grace to those around us.

In conclusion, embracing our identity in Christ involves understanding God's truth about who we are and allowing this truth to shape our thoughts and perceptions. It means overcoming negative thoughts and lies with the powerful, transforming truth of God's Word. As we allow God's truth to permeate our minds and hearts, we'll experience a newfound freedom and joy in our Christian walk, living out the abundant life Christ has promised us.

Cultivating a Biblical Mindset to Embrace Your Worth in Christ

The Bible tells us that "as a man thinks in his heart, so is he" (Proverbs 23:7, ASV). This profound piece of wisdom demonstrates the power of our thoughts and mindset in shaping who we are. As Christians, cultivating a biblical mindset is pivotal in fully embracing our worth in Christ.

The Biblical Mindset: What It Is

A biblical mindset, or a mind that is set on the things of God, is one that aligns its thoughts, beliefs, and perspectives with the truth of God's Word. It takes every thought captive, measures it against the standard of Scripture (2 Corinthians 10:5, ESV), and accepts only what is in line with God's truth.

The Role of the Bible in Shaping Our Mindset

God's Word is the ultimate source of truth; it reveals to us who God is, who we are, and how we are to live. When we saturate our minds with Scripture, it begins to shape our thinking, replace falsehoods and misconceptions with truth, and transform us into the image of Christ.

How to Cultivate a Biblical Mindset

Cultivating a biblical mindset requires intentional and consistent engagement with Scripture. Here's how to develop it:

- **Daily Reading of the Word:** Consistent exposure to Scripture is fundamental in cultivating a biblical mindset. Engage with the Bible daily, even if it means reading just a few verses at a time. "Blessed is the man who walks not in the counsel of the wicked, nor stands in the way of sinners, nor sits in the seat of scoffers; but his delight is in the law of the Lord, and on his law he meditates day and night" (Psalm 1:1-2, ESV).

- **Meditation:** Meditating on Scripture means to ponder, consider, and chew over God's Word. It involves not just reading the Word, but thinking deeply about it, applying it to our lives, and allowing it to permeate our thoughts.

- **Prayerful Engagement with Scripture:** As you read the Bible, pray that God would open your eyes to understand His Word and apply it to your life. Ask Him to reveal His truth and to help you embrace it in your life.

- **Application:** Lastly, apply God's Word in your life. Knowledge of Scripture is vital, but it's in the application of that knowledge where true transformation happens. "But be doers of the word, and not hearers only, deceiving yourselves" (James 1:22, ESV).

The Result of a Biblical Mindset

With a biblical mindset, we begin to see ourselves as God sees us. We understand our worth not based on worldly standards, but on the fact that we are God's beloved children, redeemed by Christ's sacrifice and created for His glory.

This understanding frees us from seeking approval and validation from others, liberating us to live authentically and confidently as children of God. It empowers us to reject lies and negative thoughts, embrace our identity in Christ, and live out our God-given purpose.

In conclusion, cultivating a biblical mindset is crucial in embracing our worth in Christ. It involves immersing our minds in God's Word, allowing it to shape our thinking and align our perspectives with God's truth. As we do this, we'll gain a clearer understanding of our identity in Christ and learn to embrace the priceless worth we have in Him.

Embracing God's Love and Grace

Experiencing the Unconditional Love and Forgiveness of God

The Christian journey is not just about understanding and recognizing our identity and worth in Christ, but also about experiencing the deep and profound love and forgiveness of God. This love is not like any human love we have experienced—it is unconditional, unchanging, and everlasting. Similarly, God's forgiveness is all-encompassing, utterly complete, and freely given to those who accept Jesus Christ as their Lord and Savior.

Understanding God's Unconditional Love

Unconditional love is love without strings attached. It doesn't change based on our actions or circumstances. God's love for us is exactly this. It's described in Romans 5:8 (ESV) which says, "But God shows his love for us in that while we were still sinners, Christ died for us."

This statement is powerful in its declaration. God's love is not contingent on us being 'worthy' or 'good enough'. Even while we were mired in sin, rebelling against God, He still loved us. This divine love led Him to give His one and only Son, Jesus Christ, to die on the cross for our sins, so we might be reconciled to Him.

Experiencing this love means accepting that we are loved not because of who we are or what we have done, but because of who God is. It requires us to embrace this truth deeply within our hearts, allowing it to shape our identity, our worth, and our understanding of God.

Experiencing God's Forgiveness

Alongside His unconditional love, God offers us complete forgiveness through Christ. "If we confess our sins, he is faithful and just to forgive us our sins and to cleanse us from all unrighteousness" (1 John 1:9, ESV).

God's forgiveness is total and absolute. When we repent of our sins and turn to Christ, God forgives us completely. This doesn't mean that we won't face consequences for our actions, but it does mean that we are no longer held accountable for our sins before God—they have been paid for in full by Jesus' sacrifice on the cross.

Experiencing this forgiveness is a profound moment in any believer's life. It's a moment of liberation, a release from the burden of guilt and shame. It's a moment when we understand that we are no longer defined by our past, but by God's love and grace.

Living in God's Love and Forgiveness

Living in the reality of God's love and forgiveness transforms our lives. We move from a place of guilt and shame to a place of freedom and acceptance. We realize that we are not loved because we are 'good enough', but because we are cherished by God, who created us in His image.

Moreover, recognizing and experiencing God's forgiveness helps us to forgive ourselves and others. It prompts a change in our mindset where we no longer hold on to bitterness, anger, or resentment, but instead choose to extend grace and forgiveness, just as we have received from God.

In conclusion, experiencing the unconditional love and forgiveness of God is a transformative journey. It reshapes our identity, instills us with an understanding of our true worth in Christ, and empowers us to live in freedom and grace. As we journey on this path, we discover the profound depths of God's love and mercy, and we learn to reflect these in our own lives, thereby making a difference to those around us.

Understanding the Significance of God's Grace in Shaping Our Identity

God's grace is foundational to Christian theology and crucial to our understanding of our identity in Christ. It refers to the unmerited favor and mercy that God extends to us, despite our sinfulness. God's grace is the means by which we are saved, through faith in Jesus Christ. But its significance extends far beyond our salvation—it also plays a crucial role in shaping our identity as believers.

The Gift of Grace

Grace, in essence, is a gift. Ephesians 2:8-9 (ESV) says, "For by grace you have been saved through faith. And this is not your own doing; it is the gift of God, not a result of works, so that no one may boast."

Grace is unearned and undeserved. It is bestowed upon us freely by a loving God, who gave His only Son, Jesus Christ, to die for our sins. This grace is the means by which we are justified, or declared righteous, before God. Our sins are forgiven, not because we have earned or deserved such mercy, but because of God's grace.

In understanding grace, we realize that our identity in Christ is not based on our own merit or worthiness, but on God's love and mercy. This understanding profoundly shapes our sense of self and our relationship with God.

Grace and Our Identity in Christ

Grace doesn't just impact our initial justification—it also impacts our ongoing transformation, a process known as sanctification.

Titus 2:11-12 (ESV) says, "For the grace of God has appeared, bringing salvation for all people, training us to renounce ungodliness and worldly passions, and to live self-controlled, upright, and godly lives in the present age."

This passage emphasizes that grace isn't just about forgiveness of sin; it's also about transformation of character. God's grace is constantly at work in us, enabling us to grow and mature in our Christian walk and to increasingly reflect Christ in our lives.

The concept of grace underscores that our identity in Christ isn't static. We are not just "saved sinners"; we are new creations, being continually transformed into the likeness of Christ.

Living by Grace

Living by grace means recognizing our constant dependence on God. We cannot live the Christian life in our own strength. Instead, we are reliant on God's grace, which empowers and enables us.

In 2 Corinthians 12:9 (ESV), the Apostle Paul quotes the Lord's response to his plea for help: "My grace is sufficient for you, for my power is made perfect in weakness." Paul's response to this statement is powerful: "Therefore I will boast all the more gladly of my weaknesses, so that the power of Christ may rest upon me."

Understanding and experiencing God's grace leads us to humility. We know that we are weak and sinful, yet God's power is made perfect in our weakness. This awareness not only shapes our identity—it also influences our attitudes, behaviors, and relationships.

In conclusion, God's grace plays an essential role in shaping our identity in Christ. It's the means by which we are saved and the power that enables us to live for Christ. It's the assurance of God's love and mercy towards us, despite our sinfulness. And it's the basis for our humility and dependence on God. Truly, understanding the significance of God's grace profoundly impacts our self-understanding and our relationship with God.

Living Out Your Identity in Christ

Applying Biblical Principles in Your Daily Life

An essential part of our Christian walk involves applying biblical principles to our everyday lives. As followers of Christ, we believe that the Bible is not just a collection of historical narratives, poems, and letters. It is, as 2 Timothy 3:16 (ESV) tells us, "breathed out by God and profitable for teaching, for reproof, for correction, and for training in righteousness." It is a guidebook for life that provides us with principles for living in a way that is pleasing to God and beneficial to us and those around us.

Aligning with God's Word

Living a life aligned with God's word begins with knowing what it says. Regular Bible study and prayer are vital components of this process. As we immerse ourselves in Scripture, God's principles and precepts become clear to us, and the Holy Spirit enlightens our understanding.

Joshua 1:8 (ASV) tells us, "This book of the law shall not depart out of thy mouth; but thou shalt meditate therein day and night, that thou mayest observe to do according to all that is written therein: for then thou shalt make thy way prosperous, and then thou shalt have good success."

This implies the importance of consistency in studying God's Word, meditating on it, and applying its truths to our lives. It's about more than merely reading the Bible; it's about letting its truths permeate our hearts and minds and actively living them out.

Bearing Spiritual Fruit

A crucial biblical principle is the call to bear spiritual fruit. Galatians 5:22-23 (ESV) outlines the fruit of the Spirit: "But the fruit of the Spirit is love, joy, peace, patience, kindness, goodness, faithfulness, gentleness, self-control; against such things there is no law."

Developing these qualities requires daily intentionality. It involves asking the Holy Spirit to cultivate these characteristics in us, then cooperating with His work by making conscious choices to live according to these principles. This might mean choosing to respond with patience and kindness when we're tempted to react in anger, or choosing to pursue peace, even when surrounded by conflict.

Loving God and Others

Jesus summarized the law and the prophets in two commandments: loving God and loving others. Matthew 22:37-39 (ESV) quotes Jesus as saying, "'You shall love the Lord your God with all your heart and with all your soul and with all your mind. This is the great and first commandment. And a second is like it: You shall love your neighbor as yourself.'"

Loving God involves obedience to His commands (John 14:15, ESV). Loving others means showing kindness, forgiveness, and compassion—reflecting God's love to those around us. These principles are to permeate every area of our lives, influencing our actions, attitudes, and relationships.

Walking by Faith

2 Corinthians 5:7 (ESV) says, "For we walk by faith, not by sight." Walking by faith means trusting in God's promises and His character, even when circumstances are challenging. This trust impacts our decisions and responses to life's situations, leading us to live with hope, perseverance, and confidence in God's sovereignty and goodness.

In conclusion, applying biblical principles in our daily lives involves a commitment to know and understand God's Word, a determination to live out its teachings, and a reliance on the Holy Spirit for guidance and empowerment. It's a journey that transforms us, aligns us more closely with God's will, and allows us to make a positive difference in the world.

Walking in the Confidence of Your Identity and Purpose in Christ

Understanding and embracing our identity in Christ is pivotal to our Christian journey. However, truly living out this identity with confidence and purpose requires a deeper commitment. It is not enough to merely know who we are in Christ; we must also walk boldly in this knowledge, applying it to every aspect of our lives.

Your Identity in Christ

Scripture teaches that believers in Jesus Christ are new creations. 2 Corinthians 5:17 (ESV) states, "Therefore, if anyone is in Christ, he is a new creation. The old has passed away; behold, the new has come." This transformative reality is profound. As believers, we are no longer defined by our past mistakes, our shortcomings, or the world's labels. Instead, we are defined by our relationship with Christ.

In Christ, we are redeemed, justified, and sanctified. We are loved, forgiven, and adopted into God's family. We are co-heirs with Christ, and we have the Holy Spirit dwelling within us (Romans 8:15-17, ESV). Understanding this identity is essential to walking confidently in Christ.

Your Purpose in Christ

In addition to our new identity, believers in Jesus are also given a new purpose. Jesus commissions His followers in Matthew 28:19-20

(ESV), saying, "Go therefore and make disciples of all nations, baptizing them in the name of the Father and of the Son and of the Holy Spirit, teaching them to observe all that I have commanded you."

Our purpose is twofold. First, we are called to know and love God deeply. This involves cultivating a personal relationship with Him through prayer, Bible study, and obedience. Second, we are commissioned to share God's love and truth with others, inviting them into the same transformative relationship with Christ that we enjoy.

Walking in Confidence and Purpose

Walking in the confidence of our identity and purpose in Christ requires faith and courage. It is a conscious decision to believe what God says about us and to live accordingly. It means rejecting the lies of the enemy, the world, and our sinful nature that seek to diminish our worth and derail our purpose.

The Apostle Paul provides an excellent example of this confident walk. Despite suffering, opposition, and hardship, Paul consistently affirmed his identity and purpose in Christ (Philippians 3:12-14, ESV). He did not allow circumstances, past failures, or the opinions of others to shake his confidence.

To walk confidently in our identity and purpose, we must continually align our thoughts and beliefs with God's Word. When we are tempted to doubt our worth or purpose, we can turn to Scripture for reassurance. We can also ask the Holy Spirit to affirm truth in our hearts and to empower us to live out our divine calling.

Living Out Your Identity and Purpose

Living out your identity and purpose involves applying your understanding of who you are in Christ to your everyday life. It means letting your identity shape your thoughts, attitudes, words, and actions. It also means striving to fulfill your God-given purpose through your relationships, work, ministry, and other areas of influence.

Walking confidently in our identity and purpose in Christ is not a one-time event but a lifelong journey. It requires daily surrender, continual reliance on God's grace, and a persistent commitment to live for Christ's glory. But as we walk this journey, we will experience the joy and fulfillment that come from knowing we are living in alignment with God's perfect design and purpose for us.

Overcoming Obstacles and Embracing Victory

Conquering Self-Doubt, Fear, and Insecurities through Christ

Every person, Christian or not, grapples with self-doubt, fear, and insecurities at various points in their life. These are part of the human experience, the consequences of living in a fallen world. Yet, as believers, we have a powerful resource in Christ to conquer these challenges.

The Problem of Self-Doubt, Fear, and Insecurities

These three — self-doubt, fear, and insecurities — often come together, undermining our confidence in God's promises and obstructing our ability to live out our identity and purpose in Christ. They can hinder our spiritual growth, damage our relationships, and prevent us from fulfilling God's call on our lives.

Self-doubt makes us question our worth, capabilities, and our standing before God. Fear magnifies perceived threats and potential failures, creating anxiety and discouragement. Insecurities lead us to compare ourselves unfavorably with others, fostering discontent and resentment.

These are real struggles, but they do not align with the truth of who we are in Christ. They are distortions that emerge from our fallen nature, the world's false messages, and the enemy's lies.

God's Truth to Combat Self-Doubt, Fear, and Insecurities

The first step to conquering these obstacles is to replace lies and distortions with God's truth. Scripture affirms that in Christ, we are deeply loved, fully accepted, and empowered for every good work.

For self-doubt, we need to understand and embrace our worth in Christ. Ephesians 2:10 (ESV) states, "For we are his workmanship, created in Christ Jesus for good works, which God prepared beforehand, that we should walk in them." We are not accidents, and our lives are not meaningless. God has crafted us with purpose and intentionality.

To conquer fear, we can claim God's promises of his presence, power, and peace. One such promise is found in Isaiah 41:10 (ASV), "Fear thou not, for I am with thee; be not dismayed, for I am thy God; I will strengthen thee; yea, I will help thee; yea, I will uphold thee with the right hand of my righteousness."

To overcome insecurities, we must recognize that our value is not determined by worldly standards but by our identity in Christ. Galatians 2:20 (ESV) declares, "I have been crucified with Christ. It is no longer I who live, but Christ who lives in me." Our worth is not in what we have or do, but in who we are in Christ.

Living in Victory through Christ

Knowing God's truth is one thing; living in it is another. To truly conquer self-doubt, fear, and insecurities, we need to continually align our thoughts, attitudes, and actions with God's Word.

First, we must immerse ourselves in Scripture, allowing God's Word to shape our perceptions and responses. Through regular Bible study and meditation, we can internalize God's truths and counteract the lies that fuel our self-doubt, fear, and insecurities.

Second, we should maintain an ongoing dialogue with God through prayer. We can bring our struggles to Him, ask for His wisdom and strength, and thank Him for His promises.

Third, we should surround ourselves with supportive Christian community. Fellow believers can encourage us, pray for us, and remind us of God's truth when we are struggling.

Finally, we must practice living out our identity and purpose in Christ. As we take steps of faith, depending on God's grace and power, we will experience His faithfulness and grow in confidence.

Concluding Thoughts

Conquering self-doubt, fear, and insecurities is not a quick or easy process. It's a lifelong journey that requires commitment, perseverance, and continual reliance on God's grace. But as we engage in this journey, we can experience increasing freedom, joy, and fulfillment, knowing that we are living in alignment with our true identity and purpose in Christ.

Embracing Victory in Christ and Living Out Your Full Potential

Christianity is a faith not of defeat but of victory. Christ's work on the cross overcame the world, and as His followers, we too can embrace this victory in our lives. Yet, living victoriously in Christ is not merely about overcoming sin or enduring trials; it is about living out our full potential in Christ, maximizing the gifts, talents, and opportunities God has given us for His glory and the benefit of others.

Understanding Victory in Christ

Christ's victory on the cross was comprehensive. He conquered sin, death, and the power of the enemy. As Christians, we are not only beneficiaries of Christ's victory, but participants in it as well. Romans 8:37 (ESV) affirms, "In all these things we are more than conquerors through him who loved us."

Victory in Christ is both a positional and experiential reality. Positionally, we are already victorious in Christ. Ephesians 2:6 (ESV) tells us that God "raised us up with him and seated us with him in the heavenly places in Christ Jesus." This is our permanent status as believers.

Experientially, we live out this victory in our daily lives as we walk in obedience to God's Word, overcome sin, endure trials, and bear fruit for God's Kingdom. This is a dynamic process, involving ongoing dependence on God's grace and power.

Living Out Your Full Potential in Christ

Living out our full potential in Christ means using all that God has given us — our gifts, talents, time, resources, and opportunities —

for His glory and the benefit of others. It involves seeking God's will, walking in obedience, and being faithful stewards of all that He has entrusted to us.

1 Peter 4:10 (ESV) says, "As each has received a gift, use it to serve one another, as good stewards of God's varied grace." This verse highlights two key principles for living out our full potential in Christ.

First, we should use our gifts to serve others. God has uniquely equipped each of us with certain abilities and skills. These are not meant for our personal gain, but for the edification of the body of Christ and the furtherance of God's Kingdom.

Second, we should be good stewards of God's grace. Stewardship is about responsible management. It involves recognizing that all we have is from God, and therefore, should be used in a way that honors Him.

Practical Steps for Embracing Victory and Living Out Your Full Potential in Christ

1. **Know who you are in Christ**: Understand your identity and worth in Christ, as revealed in Scripture. Internalize the truth that you are deeply loved, fully accepted, and empowered for every good work in Christ.

2. **Live out your identity in Christ**: Make choices that reflect your identity and values as a Christian. Avoid things that compromise your faith or hinder your walk with God.

3. **Seek God's will**: Regularly spend time in prayer and Bible study, asking God for wisdom and guidance in all areas of your life.

4. **Use your gifts for God's glory**: Identify your gifts and talents and find ways to use them for God's Kingdom. This could involve serving in your local church, participating in mission work, or using your professional skills to make a positive impact in your community.

5. **Practice good stewardship**: Manage your time, resources, and opportunities in a way that honors God. This involves being disciplined, wise, and generous.

Concluding Thoughts

Embracing victory in Christ and living out your full potential is a lifelong journey. It requires intentionality, perseverance, and dependence on God's grace. But as we engage in this journey, we can experience the joy of living a life of purpose, knowing that we are making a difference for God's Kingdom.

Walking in God's Purpose for Your Life

Discovering and Fulfilling Your Unique Calling and Purpose

Every Christian is called by God to a unique purpose. This calling, though it may take on various forms, is grounded in the great commission, given to us by Jesus Himself in Matthew 28:19-20 (ESV): "Go therefore and make disciples of all nations, baptizing them in the name of the Father and of the Son and of the Holy Spirit, teaching them to observe all that I have commanded you." This is our overarching calling—to make disciples. However, how each person fulfills this calling is unique to their God-given gifts, life situation, and specific purpose.

Discovering Your Unique Calling

The first step in fulfilling your unique purpose is to discover it. The discovery process involves prayer, the study of God's Word, self-assessment, and seeking wise counsel from mature believers. It is important to keep in mind that God is the One who calls us and He is faithful to reveal His specific purpose for our lives when we earnestly seek Him.

As you pray and read the Bible, ask God for insight into your calling. Jeremiah 33:3 (ESV) encourages us: "Call to me and I will answer you, and will tell you great and hidden things that you have not known."

A self-assessment is a practical way of identifying your strengths, passions, and spiritual gifts. The Apostle Paul, in Romans 12:6-8 (ESV), mentions different gifts given to us: "Having gifts that differ according to the grace given to us, let us use them: if prophecy, in proportion to our faith; if service, in our serving; the one who teaches, in his teaching...". Understanding your gifts can provide clues to your calling.

Finally, seek counsel from mature believers—those who are grounded in their faith and who exhibit the wisdom that comes from walking with the Lord over time. They may be able to provide insight into your life that you may have overlooked.

Fulfilling Your Unique Purpose

Once you have a sense of your unique calling, the next step is to begin living it out. This involves several key elements:

1. **Prayerful planning:** Begin by asking God to guide your steps. As Proverbs 16:9 (ESV) reminds us, "The heart of man plans his way, but the Lord establishes his steps." Develop a vision for how you might fulfill your purpose, setting specific, measurable, attainable, relevant, and time-bound (SMART) goals that align with your calling.

2. **Obedient action:** Faith without works is dead (James 2:17, ESV). Once you have a plan, begin taking steps to implement it. This could involve pursuing further education or training, looking for opportunities to serve in your local church or community, or even transitioning to a new career that better aligns with your calling.

3. **Persistent endurance:** Fulfilling your calling is often a long-term endeavor, filled with challenges and obstacles. The Apostle Paul encourages us in Galatians 6:9 (ESV), "And let us not grow weary of doing good, for in due season we will reap, if we do not give up."

4. **Continuous learning:** As you journey toward fulfilling your unique calling, always remain open to learning and growing. Regularly spend time in God's Word, and continually seek His guidance. Also, consider finding a mentor who can provide encouragement, wisdom, and accountability along the way.

Conclusion

Discovering and fulfilling your unique calling and purpose is an exciting, life-long journey. It is about co-laboring with God in His redemptive work in the world. As we seek God's will, use our gifts and abilities in service to Him, and persist in the face of challenges, we can have confidence that we are making a difference for His Kingdom. In the words of Paul in 1 Corinthians 15:58 (ESV): "Therefore, my beloved brothers, be steadfast, immovable, always abounding in the work of the Lord, knowing that in the Lord your labor is not in vain."

Using Your Gifts and Talents to Impact Others and Bring Glory to God

The Christian faith encourages us to leverage our unique gifts and talents, not only for personal satisfaction or worldly success but more importantly, for the glorification of God and the betterment of others. This principle is deeply rooted in the biblical narrative and can significantly shape our identity and purpose as believers.

The Biblical Perspective on Gifts and Talents

Scripture affirms that every believer has been gifted by God in unique and significant ways. In 1 Corinthians 12:4-7 (ESV), Paul states, "Now there are varieties of gifts, but the same Spirit; and there are varieties of service, but the same Lord; and there are varieties of activities, but it is the same God who empowers them all in everyone. To each is given the manifestation of the Spirit for the common good."

This passage underscores two fundamental truths about our gifts and talents. First, they are given to us by God and empowered by Him. Second, these gifts and talents are given to us for a reason—to contribute to the common good.

Impacting Others with Your Gifts and Talents

One significant way we fulfill our God-given purpose is by using our gifts and talents to positively impact the lives of others. Whether it's through acts of service, teaching, encouragement, giving, or any number of other possibilities, our gifts can make a real difference.

In the Parable of the Talents in Matthew 25:14-30 (ESV), Jesus illustrates the importance of using our talents wisely. The servants who put their talents to use were rewarded, while the one who hid his talent was rebuked. This parable is a powerful reminder that we are called to actively use what God has given us, not hide it away.

Bringing Glory to God with Your Gifts and Talents

However, using our gifts and talents isn't just about benefiting others. It's also about bringing glory to God. In 1 Peter 4:10-11 (ESV), we're told, "As each has received a gift, use it to serve one another, as good stewards of God's varied grace... in order that in everything God may be glorified through Jesus Christ."

By using our gifts and talents to serve others, we demonstrate the love of Christ in practical ways and reflect His character to the world, thereby glorifying God. Our gifts and talents, then, become a conduit through which God's glory is revealed.

The Pursuit of Excellence

While it's essential to use our gifts and talents, it's equally important to strive for excellence in doing so. Paul encourages us in Colossians 3:23-24 (ESV), "Whatever you do, work heartily, as for the Lord and not for men... You are serving the Lord Christ." When we approach our work—whatever it might be—with this attitude, we bring honor to God and become effective ambassadors for Christ.

Conclusion

As believers, our identity in Christ calls us to a life of purpose—a life where we use our God-given gifts and talents to impact others and bring glory to God. This is an integral part of our Christian walk, enabling us to make a real difference in the world while honoring our

Creator. So, may we step out in faith, using our unique abilities to serve others and shine the light of Christ in all we do.

APPENDIX C Overcoming Self-Doubt with God's Promises: Embracing Your Potential

The Power of God's Promises

Understanding the Significance and Reliability of God's Promises

As Christians, our faith journey is deeply interwoven with the promises of God revealed in Scripture. We take comfort in His assurances, lean on His covenants, and find strength in His commitment to fulfill what He has proclaimed. Indeed, understanding the significance and reliability of God's promises is a critical aspect of navigating life's uncertainties and overcoming self-doubt.

The Significance of God's Promises

At their core, the promises of God reveal His character—His love, mercy, faithfulness, and righteousness. They offer a glimpse into His divine plan for humanity and form a basis for our hope and faith.

Consider the promise found in Jeremiah 29:11 (ESV): "For I know the plans I have for you, declares the Lord, plans for welfare and not for evil, to give you a future and a hope." This profound promise underscores God's caring, thoughtful, and forward-looking nature, assuring us that He has our best interests at heart, even amidst life's trials and challenges.

Promises such as this one are not just comforting words. They're significant, powerful declarations that give us insight into who God is, how He operates, and what His intentions are toward His creation.

The Reliability of God's Promises

The reliability of God's promises is rooted in His immutable nature. God, by definition, is unchanging, trustworthy, and faithful. He is not like humans, who can change their minds or fail to fulfill their promises.

In Numbers 23:19 (ASV), we are reminded of this characteristic of God: "God is not a man, that he should lie, nor a son of man, that he should repent: hath he said, and shall he not do it? Or hath he spoken, and shall he not make it good?" This passage affirms that when God makes a promise, He will surely fulfill it. We can bank on it.

One of the most profound examples of this reliability is found in the promise of the Messiah. From the time of the fall in Genesis, God promised redemption through a Savior. Despite the centuries that passed, God fulfilled this promise through Jesus Christ, as attested in the New Testament.

Overcoming Self-Doubt with God's Promises

God's promises are an effective remedy for self-doubt. When we feel insecure or unsure about our abilities, futures, or worth, we can turn to God's promises for reassurance. Philippians 4:13 (ESV) tells us, "I can do all things through him who strengthens me." This promise can empower us to overcome self-doubt, knowing that God equips us with the strength we need to accomplish our God-given tasks and responsibilities.

Further, when we grapple with feelings of insignificance or unworthiness, we can lean on promises such as Psalm 139:14 (ASV), which affirms, "I will give thanks unto thee; for I am fearfully and wonderfully made: Wonderful are thy works; And that my soul knoweth right well."

Conclusion

The promises of God serve as a guiding light in our Christian walk, illuminating our paths, strengthening our faith, and fortifying our identities in Christ. As we grasp the significance and reliability of these divine assurances, we are better equipped to overcome self-doubt and embrace our full potential. So, let's anchor ourselves in God's promises, for they reflect His unchanging character and unwavering commitment to us, His children.

Discovering the Transformative Impact of His Word on Our Self-Doubt

The Word of God holds incredible power. It is not merely a collection of stories, laws, and prophecies, but it is living and active, with a profound impact on our lives, including how we handle self-doubt. This section explores the transformative effect of God's Word in mitigating self-doubt and how we can use it to embrace our God-given potential.

The Living Word and Self-Doubt

The Bible is often referred to as the living Word. In Hebrews 4:12 (ESV), it is described as "living and active, sharper than any two-edged sword, piercing to the division of soul and of spirit, of joints and of marrow, and discerning the thoughts and intentions of the heart." These words portray the Bible as more than just a book. It's a dynamic, transformative tool with the power to penetrate our hearts and minds, reveal truth, and provoke change.

When it comes to self-doubt, the Word of God serves as an illuminating mirror, reflecting the reality of who we are in Christ, helping us discern truth from lie, and challenging the negative self-perceptions that often fuel our insecurities.

The Impact of the Word on Self-Doubt

God's Word has a transformative impact on self-doubt through two significant ways: through identity affirmation and truth revelation.

Identity Affirmation: The Word of God is rich with affirmations of our identity in Christ. Verses like Ephesians 2:10 (ESV), which states, "For we are his workmanship, created in Christ Jesus for good works, which God prepared beforehand, that we should walk in them," remind us that we are purposefully crafted by God. Such affirmations, when internalized, help counter feelings of self-doubt, reminding us of our inherent worth and God-given purpose.

Truth Revelation: God's Word exposes the falsehoods that often feed our self-doubt. When we find ourselves doubting our capabilities or worth, the Word of God can dispel these misconceptions. For example, when we fear our mistakes are too great, the Word reminds us, "If we confess our sins, he is faithful and just to forgive us our sins and to cleanse us from all unrighteousness" (1 John 1:9, ESV). Such divine truths counter the lies that breed self-doubt.

Applying the Word to Overcome Self-Doubt

Knowing the transformative power of God's Word is one thing; applying it is another. Here are some practical steps to leverage the Word in overcoming self-doubt:

Consistent Study and Meditation: Regularly reading and reflecting on God's Word is fundamental. The more we immerse ourselves in the Scriptures, the more we absorb its truths, which can then counteract self-doubt. Psalm 1:2-3 (ASV) illustrates the blessing of the one who delights in the law of the Lord and meditates on His law day and night.

Memorization: By memorizing key Scriptures, we equip ourselves with a ready arsenal of truth to combat self-doubt as it arises. These verses serve as immediate reminders of our worth, potential, and identity in Christ.

Prayer: Praying the Scriptures is a powerful way to internalize God's promises and truths. By praying the Word, we engage in a personal dialogue with God about His promises and truths, helping to move them from head knowledge to heart conviction.

Conclusion

The Word of God is not a passive, inert text but a vibrant, living instrument of transformation. As we consistently engage with it, internalizing its truths and promises, we can dismantle self-doubt and more fully embrace our identity and potential in Christ. The transformative impact of His Word offers us a mighty tool in the quest to overcome self-doubt and live in the confidence of our God-given worth and purpose. Let's continue to delve into and apply His Word, allowing it to mold us, shape us, and fortify us against the debilitating power of self-doubt.

Identifying and Challenging Self-Doubt

Recognizing the Roots and Manifestations of Self-Doubt in Our Lives

In our journey towards overcoming self-doubt, it is essential first to recognize its roots and how it manifests in our lives. Self-doubt, like any other internal struggle, is complex, often intertwined with various aspects of our life experiences, personal beliefs, and external influences. This section provides an exploration of the origins of self-doubt and how it typically reveals itself in our lives.

The Roots of Self-Doubt

The roots of self-doubt often reach deep into our past experiences and learned beliefs. Let's explore some of the most common sources:

Past Experiences: Negative experiences, particularly those involving failure or criticism, can plant seeds of self-doubt. An individual who frequently encountered criticism or failure, particularly during formative years, might develop a pattern of doubting their abilities or worth.

Unrealistic Expectations: Society, family, and even the church sometimes set high, sometimes unattainable, standards for success, spirituality, or behavior. Struggling to meet these expectations can foster self-doubt.

Comparison: Comparing oneself to others is a common source of self-doubt. In an age where social media highlights others' successes, it's easy to feel inadequate or doubt our worth or abilities.

Spiritual Warfare: The Bible also speaks of self-doubt as a tool that the enemy uses to hinder believers' effectiveness. The apostle Peter warns in 1 Peter 5:8 (ESV), "Be sober-minded; be watchful. Your adversary the devil prowls around like a roaring lion, seeking someone to devour."

Manifestations of Self-Doubt

Self-doubt can manifest in various ways, impacting different aspects of our lives. Here are some of the common ways self-doubt may reveal itself:

Hesitation and Procrastination: Self-doubt often leads to a lack of confidence in making decisions or taking action. This can result in constant hesitation or procrastination.

Perfectionism: Ironically, self-doubt can sometimes drive individuals to be perfectionists, continually striving to meet unrealistic standards to validate their worth or abilities.

Low Self-Esteem: Persistent self-doubt often erodes self-esteem, leading to a chronic sense of inadequacy.

Overdependence on Others: Self-doubt can also lead to an unhealthy reliance on others' opinions or approval, given the individual's lack of trust in their judgment or abilities.

Imposter Syndrome: This involves feeling like a fraud, doubting one's accomplishments, and having a persistent fear of being exposed as inadequate or unqualified, despite evidence to the contrary.

Conclusion

Recognizing the roots and manifestations of self-doubt is a crucial first step towards overcoming it. Once we understand where our self-doubt originates and how it influences our behavior, we can more effectively counter it with God's truth. The Psalmist's words in Psalm 139:23-24 (ASV), "Search me, O God, and know my heart... see if there be any wicked way in me, and lead me in the way everlasting," highlight the need for this self-examination and reliance on God's guidance. With this awareness and God's Word, we can start to dismantle self-doubt and step into the full potential of who we are in Christ.

Confronting Negative Thoughts and Beliefs with God's Truth

When self-doubt has rooted itself deeply in our hearts and minds, it may seem a Herculean task to uproot it and replace it with self-assurance and trust in God. Nonetheless, the Bible assures us that it is not only possible but within our grasp through the application of

God's truth in confronting these negative thoughts and beliefs. We need to hold the shield of faith against the arrows of negativity and self-doubt (Ephesians 6:16, ESV).

Understanding the Influence of Negative Thoughts

Our thoughts hold immense power over our lives. They form the foundation of our beliefs, steer our actions, and shape our relationships. Proverbs 4:23 (ASV) asserts, "Keep thy heart with all diligence; for out of it are the issues of life." The Bible consistently underscores the connection between our thoughts and the quality of our lives, signaling the need for vigilance over the contents of our minds.

Self-doubt emerges when we entertain thoughts of inadequacy, failure, and insignificance. Such thoughts can stem from various sources, including past failures, negative experiences, harsh words spoken by others, and our own insecurities. If left unaddressed, these thoughts germinate into beliefs that can undermine our self-worth, discourage us from pursuing our goals, and even lead us away from God's purpose for our lives.

Identifying and Countering Negative Thoughts with God's Word

God's Word serves as an antidote to the venom of self-doubt. It contains the unchanging truth about who we are in Christ, our worth to God, and His promises for our lives. We find in it the affirmation that we are "fearfully and wonderfully made" (Psalm 139:14, ESV) and that we can do all things through Christ who strengthens us (Philippians 4:13, ESV). These are but a few examples of the powerful truths that can combat negative self-perception and self-doubt.

By regularly reading, studying, and meditating on the Scriptures, we can equip ourselves with a reservoir of God's truths. We can then draw from this reservoir whenever negative thoughts attempt to invade our minds. This practice can help us transform our thinking and align our beliefs with God's truth.

To confront our negative thoughts, we first have to identify them. These could be thoughts about our worth, our abilities, or our future.

They often stem from self-doubt, fear, past experiences, or lies that we've been led to believe.

Once we've identified these thoughts, the next step is to counter them with God's truth. This process is not about positive thinking or merely replacing negative thoughts with positive ones. Instead, it's about replacing the lies we've believed with the truth found in God's Word.

Here are some examples of this process:

Lie: "I'm not good enough."

Truth: "I am fearfully and wonderfully made" (Psalm 139:14, ESV).

Lie: "I can't do this."

Truth: "I can do all things through him who strengthens me" (Philippians 4:13, ESV).

Lie: "I'm a failure."

Truth: "The righteous may fall seven times but still get up" (Proverbs 24:16, ESV).

Each time a negative thought arises, we can choose to confront it with these truths. As we consistently apply this practice, our minds begin to shift from a place of self-doubt to one of faith and confidence in who God says we are.

The Importance of Prayer

In this battle against negative thoughts and self-doubt, prayer is our line of communication with God, our Commander-in-Chief. Through prayer, we can seek His wisdom and strength, ask Him to shine His light on the areas of our hearts and minds where negativity lurks, and request His help in replacing these negative thoughts with His truth.

Just as King David prayed in Psalm 139:23-24 (ESV), we too can ask God to "Search me, O God, and know my heart! Try me and know my thoughts! And see if there be any grievous way in me, and lead me in the way everlasting!"

Harnessing the Power of God's Word

The power of God's Word lies not merely in its ability to counteract negative thoughts but also in its capacity to transform our lives. Hebrews 4:12 (ESV) tells us that "the word of God is living and active, sharper than any two-edged sword, piercing to the division of soul and of spirit, of joints and of marrow, and discerning the thoughts and intentions of the heart."

As we marinate our minds in the Word of God, we allow His truth to penetrate our thinking and alter our perspectives. Over time, this process of mind renewal enables us to overcome self-doubt and step into the confidence of knowing who we are in Christ.

The Role of Prayer and the Holy Spirit

The task of renewing our minds and confronting negative thoughts can be daunting. It requires consistent effort and honesty with ourselves. Fortunately, we are not left to do this alone. The Holy Spirit, our helper, empowers us and guides us in this journey.

Prayer plays an essential role here. Through prayer, we ask God to reveal any harmful beliefs we've held onto and ask for His help in replacing these with His truth. It's through prayer that we express our dependence on God, acknowledging that without Him, our efforts would be in vain.

We can echo the plea of Psalm 139:23-24 (ESV), which says, "Search me, O God, and know my heart! Try me and know my thoughts! And see if there be any grievous way in me, and lead me in the way everlasting!"

The Power of God's Word in Confronting Negative Thoughts

As Hebrews 4:12 (ESV) declares, "For the word of God is living and active, sharper than any two-edged sword, piercing to the division of soul and of spirit, of joints and of marrow, and discerning the thoughts and intentions of the heart."

God's Word is a powerful tool in combating negative thoughts and self-doubt. It's not just a collection of ancient writings but a living, dynamic force that penetrates our hearts and minds, exposing our deepest thoughts and desires.

When we read and meditate on God's Word, we allow His truth to infiltrate our minds, dispelling lies and falsehoods. We allow the light of God's Word to illuminate our inner beings, revealing areas where our thinking needs to be aligned with His.

The Process of Mind Renewal

Renewing our minds is a continuous process. It's not a one-time event, but a daily, even hourly, practice. It involves choosing God's truth over our feelings or perceptions, allowing His Word to shape our beliefs and, consequently, our behaviors and decisions.

Paul admonishes us in Romans 12:2 (ESV), "Do not be conformed to this world, but be transformed by the renewal of your mind, that by testing you may discern what is the will of God, what is good and acceptable and perfect."

As we confront our negative thoughts with God's truth, we undergo a transformation. We're no longer bound by self-doubt or ruled by fear. Instead, we're set free to live confidently in the identity that God has given us, moving forward in His promises.

Conclusion

The battle against self-doubt begins in the mind. By harnessing the power of God's Word and countering negative thoughts with His truth, we can overcome self-doubt and embrace the identity God has given us. This process involves an ongoing commitment to mind renewal through Bible study, meditation, and prayer. It may be challenging, but with the Holy Spirit as our guide and God's truth as our weapon, we can triumph over self-doubt and live out our God-given potential to the fullest. Self-doubt can be debilitating, but it doesn't have to define us. By identifying our negative thoughts and countering them with God's truth, we can dismantle self-doubt and replace it with a confidence rooted in God's promises. Armed with the truth of His Word and aided by the Holy Spirit, we can overcome the lies we've believed and step into the fullness of our identity in Christ. Our thoughts, aligned with God's truth, become a powerful force in our lives, propelling us towards fulfilling our unique purpose and potential.

Claiming God's Promises of Identity and Worth

Embracing Our Identity as God's Beloved Children

An essential part of overcoming self-doubt is recognizing and embracing our identity as God's beloved children. This requires us to understand what Scripture says about our place in God's family, and how this identity shapes our self-perception, relationships, and mission in life. It is only in the light of God's Word that we can truly see ourselves as we are: dearly loved, infinitely valuable, and purposed for His glory.

Understanding Our Identity in Christ

Firstly, we must establish that our identity is not self-created, nor is it determined by our accomplishments, our failures, or the opinions of others. Our true identity is given by God and rooted in Christ. As believers, we are not simply individuals striving to do good in this world; we are God's children, adopted into His family through the sacrificial work of Jesus Christ. The Apostle Paul affirms this in Ephesians 1:5 (ESV), stating that God "predestined us for adoption to himself as sons through Jesus Christ, according to the purpose of his will."

Furthermore, as God's children, we are loved with an immeasurable and unchanging love. Romans 8:38-39 (ESV) assures us, "For I am sure that neither death nor life, nor angels nor rulers, nor things present nor things to come, nor powers, nor height nor depth, nor anything else in all creation, will be able to separate us from the love of God in Christ Jesus our Lord." This divine love is not dependent on our performance, our goodness, or our worthiness. It is a steadfast love anchored in God's nature.

Accepting God's Love and Our Identity as His Children

Accepting this truth can be a challenge, especially for those who struggle with self-doubt. Negative experiences, past failures, and unkind words from others may cause us to question our worth and doubt God's love for us. However, we must remember that our feelings do not dictate truth. God's Word is the ultimate source of truth, and it declares that we are loved and valued by Him.

Embracing our identity as God's children means accepting His love for us and living in the assurance of that love. It means letting go of the lies that fuel our self-doubt and holding onto God's truth. It means seeing ourselves through God's eyes and allowing His perspective to shape our self-perception.

Living Out Our Identity as God's Beloved Children

Finally, embracing our identity as God's children shapes how we live our lives. It means we are not merely passers-by in this world but ambassadors of Christ, called to reflect His love and light (2 Corinthians 5:20, ESV). It means our worth is not tied to what we achieve but to Whose we are. This understanding enables us to move beyond self-doubt and step into the confident assurance that we are children of the Most High God.

Our identity in Christ also equips us to make a difference in the world. As God's children, we are commissioned to love others as He has loved us (John 15:12, ESV). This extends to how we interact with others, how we serve in our communities, and how we handle challenges and opportunities.

In conclusion, overcoming self-doubt involves embracing our identity as God's beloved children. It's about holding on to His promises, standing firm in His love, and living out our God-given potential. When self-doubt seeks to cripple us, we can rest in the truth that we are dearly loved by God and destined for His glory. As Romans 8:17 (ESV) affirms, "...if children, then heirs—heirs of God and fellow heirs with Christ, provided we suffer with him in order that we may also be glorified with him."

Anchoring Our Worth in Christ and His Redemptive Work

Overcoming self-doubt requires us to shift our focus from our perceived inadequacies and failures to the life-changing reality of Christ's redemptive work. This process involves understanding and internalizing the truth that our worth is not derived from our performance or the approval of others but anchored solely in Christ. Our value is unchangeable because it is rooted in God's unchanging love for us, demonstrated through Christ's sacrifice on the cross.

Understanding Our Worth in Christ

We live in a world that often determines our value by our successes, our appearance, our social status, or even the number of "likes" or "followers" we accumulate on social media platforms. These are fleeting and fickle measures of worth, and using them as our value anchors can lead to feelings of inadequacy and self-doubt.

However, the Bible presents a radically different perspective on our worth. It teaches us that our value is intrinsically tied to our identity in Christ. When we understand that our worth is not a result of what we do but who we are in Christ, we begin to experience freedom from the crippling effects of self-doubt.

Ephesians 2:10 (ESV) tells us that "we are his workmanship, created in Christ Jesus for good works, which God prepared beforehand, that we should walk in them." This verse reassures us that we are God's masterpiece, designed with a unique purpose that only we can fulfill. We are not accidents, but intentionally crafted by a loving Creator.

The Impact of Christ's Redemptive Work on Our Self-Worth

Christ's redemptive work at Calvary further underscores our immeasurable worth in God's eyes. Jesus' sacrifice on the cross was the ultimate demonstration of God's love for us. The Apostle Paul writes in Romans 5:8 (ESV), "but God shows his love for us in that while we were still sinners, Christ died for us." Even in our most broken state, we were so valuable to God that He sent His only Son to die for us.

The cross is the intersection of our greatest need and God's greatest love. It not only addresses our sin problem but also reveals our true worth. If we ever doubt our value, we need only to look to the cross where Christ's redemptive work was completed.

Living in the Light of Our Worth in Christ

Knowing that our worth is anchored in Christ and His redemptive work can change how we navigate life. Instead of being swayed by the ever-changing standards of the world, we stand firm in the knowledge of our unchanging value in God's eyes.

This truth brings confidence, not in ourselves, but in the God who chose to love us, redeem us, and purpose us for His glory. When self-doubt arises, we combat it by reminding ourselves of who we are in Christ and what He has done for us. We remember that we are not defined by our shortcomings, but by God's boundless grace.

In conclusion, anchoring our worth in Christ and His redemptive work is a crucial step towards overcoming self-doubt. As we daily choose to embrace this biblical truth, we can move from self-doubt to faith, from insecurity to confidence, and from fear to boldness, fully assured of our identity and worth in Christ. As Paul declared in Galatians 2:20 (ESV), "I have been crucified with Christ. It is no longer I who live, but Christ who lives in me. And the life I now live in the flesh I live by faith in the Son of God, who loved me and gave himself for me." With this assurance, we can step into the fullness of God's purposes for our lives, truly making a difference.

Renewing Your Mind through Scripture

Meditating on and Memorizing God's Promises to Combat Self-Doubt

The practice of meditating on and memorizing God's promises is an effective strategy to overcome self-doubt and embrace your God-given potential. God's Word is filled with promises that can uplift us, give us hope, and reshape our thinking to align with God's truth. Armed with these divine promises, we can counter every doubt with faith, every lie with truth, and every fear with hope.

Why Meditate on God's Promises?

Meditation is a biblical practice that involves deep reflection on God's Word. Unlike the eastern concept of meditation, which focuses on emptying the mind, Christian meditation seeks to fill the mind with God's truth. It's a time of quietness and stillness before God where we mull over His words and allow them to shape our thinking and our lives.

Psalm 1:2 (ASV) describes the blessed person as one whose "delight is in the law of Jehovah, and on his law doth he meditate day and night." Meditating on God's promises allows us to immerse ourselves in God's truths, which serve as an antidote to self-doubt.

Why Memorize God's Promises?

Memorization is another powerful spiritual discipline that helps us internalize God's promises. Psalm 119:11 (ESV) states, "I have stored up your word in my heart, that I might not sin against you." Memorizing Scripture helps us to recall and apply God's promises in our everyday life, particularly during those moments when self-doubt tries to paralyze us.

Meditating on and Memorizing God's Promises

Here's a practical way to meditate on and memorize God's promises:

1. **Choose a Promise**: Select a verse that speaks to an area where you're experiencing self-doubt. It could be a promise about God's love for you, His power to help you, or His plan for your life.

2. **Read and Reflect**: Read the verse slowly, multiple times. Reflect on each word, pondering its significance. Ask the Holy Spirit to enlighten your understanding.

3. **Memorize**: Use repetition, visualization, or even set the verse to a melody. The goal is to engrain this promise into your heart and mind.

4. **Apply**: Consider how the promise applies to your current situation. Let it guide your decisions, shape your perspective, and fuel your faith.

5. **Recall**: Throughout the day, bring this verse to mind. Let it be your weapon against self-doubt, your source of courage, and your anchor of hope.

Consider these promises as a starting point:

- **Isaiah 41:10 (ESV)**: "So do not fear, for I am with you; do not be dismayed, for I am your God. I will strengthen you and help you; I will uphold you with my righteous right hand."
- **Jeremiah 29:11 (ESV)**: "For I know the plans I have for you, declares the LORD, plans for welfare and not for evil, to give you a future and a hope."
- **Philippians 4:13 (ESV)**: "I can do all things through him who strengthens me."
- **Romans 8:37 (ESV)**: "In all these things we are more than conquerors through him who loved us."

In summary, meditating on and memorizing God's promises is a powerful practice to combat self-doubt and embrace our potential in Christ. As we fill our minds and hearts with God's Word, we equip ourselves with divine truth that empowers us to stand against the lies of self-doubt and walk in faith and confidence in God's promises.

Allowing His Word to Shape Our Thoughts and Beliefs About Ourselves

In overcoming self-doubt, it is crucial to allow God's Word to shape our thoughts and beliefs about ourselves. Our mind is a battlefield, and the weapons we use to fight the battle matter significantly. God's Word, filled with His promises and truths, is the sword of the Spirit (Ephesians 6:17, ESV), our primary weapon against self-doubt and its consequential negative thinking.

God's Word: The Source of Truth

The foundation of this process is recognizing that God's Word is the ultimate source of truth. 2 Timothy 3:16 (ESV) affirms, "All Scripture is breathed out by God and profitable for teaching, for reproof, for correction, and for training in righteousness." This verse encapsulates the authority and the inerrancy of the Bible, meaning it is free from error and is entirely reliable. Therefore, the truths we find in Scripture should shape our understanding of ourselves and the world.

Transforming Our Mindset with God's Word

To allow His Word to shape our thoughts and beliefs, we must immerse ourselves in Scripture. It involves regularly reading, meditating, and memorizing Scripture and applying it to our daily lives. As we do this, we internalize His truth, and it begins to influence our thoughts and beliefs about ourselves.

For instance, when the thought "I am not enough" creeps in, we can counter it with God's Word: "I am fearfully and wonderfully made" (Psalm 139:14, ESV). When self-doubt whispers, "I cannot handle this situation," we remind ourselves of Philippians 4:13 (ESV), "I can do all things through him who strengthens me."

In essence, we are engaging in what Romans 12:2 (ESV) describes as the renewing of the mind: "Do not be conformed to this world, but be transformed by the renewal of your mind, that by testing you may discern what is the will of God, what is good and acceptable and perfect." This renewal process involves replacing lies and negative thoughts with God's truth.

Embracing Our Identity in Christ

An essential aspect of allowing God's Word to shape our thoughts and beliefs is understanding and embracing our identity in Christ. The Bible is clear about who we are in Christ: we are God's children (John 1:12, ESV), we are new creations (2 Corinthians 5:17, ESV), and we are chosen, royal, and holy (1 Peter 2:9, ESV).

When we internalize these truths, we begin to see ourselves not as the world sees us, or as self-doubt would have us believe, but as God sees us. This shift in perspective can have a profound impact on overcoming self-doubt.

In Conclusion

Allowing God's Word to shape our thoughts and beliefs is an ongoing process. It requires time, discipline, and patience. But as we consistently engage in this process, we find that self-doubt loses its grip on us. As God's Word takes root in our hearts and minds, it reshapes our thinking, redefines our identity, and revitalizes our faith. And in this transformed mindset, we find the strength and courage to embrace our potential and make a difference for God's glory.

Walking in Faith and Confidence

Trusting in God's Promises for Our Future and Purpose

When self-doubt seeks to undermine our confidence, remembering and trusting in God's promises for our future and purpose can be a powerful way to combat it. The Bible, being the inspired, inerrant Word of God, is filled with assurances of God's plan for His people. These promises provide a firm foundation upon which we can anchor our faith and strengthen our resolve.

God's Promises for Our Future

Throughout the Scriptures, God assures us that He has a plan for our future. Jeremiah 29:11 (ESV) is a beloved verse that highlights this promise: "For I know the plans I have for you, declares the Lord, plans for welfare and not for evil, to give you a future and a hope." This verse is not a guarantee of a life free from challenges. Instead, it is a promise that God, in His sovereignty, has a plan for us and that this plan is ultimately for our good and His glory.

Another promise for our future is found in Romans 8:28 (ESV): "And we know that for those who love God all things work together for good, for those who are called according to his purpose." Even when we can't see it, God is working all things — including our doubts, struggles, and trials — for our good.

God's Promises for Our Purpose

God not only promises a future for us, but He also assures us of a purpose. In Ephesians 2:10 (ESV), we learn that "we are his workmanship, created in Christ Jesus for good works, which God prepared beforehand, that we should walk in them." Our lives have a divine purpose — to accomplish the good works God has prepared for us. As we embrace this purpose, self-doubt begins to lose its grip.

Trusting in God's Promises

Understanding God's promises is one thing; trusting in them is another. Trust involves choosing faith over fear, even when circumstances seem overwhelming. It requires believing that God is faithful to His Word, even when doubts creep in.

Practically, trusting in God's promises can involve several practices:

1. Regularly reading and studying Scripture to remind ourselves of God's promises.
2. Meditating on His promises and applying them to our circumstances.
3. Praying for faith to trust in God's promises.
4. Seeking godly counsel and encouragement from others who can remind us of God's faithfulness.

Conclusion

In overcoming self-doubt, we must remember that our feelings do not define us or our future — God's promises do. And He promises us a future and a purpose. As we trust in these promises, we can face self-doubt with faith, confidence, and the assurance that God is for us, has a plan for us, and will fulfill His purpose in us. In this way, we can truly embrace our potential and make a difference in the world for His glory.

Stepping Out in Faith and Embracing Our True Potential in Christ

Having recognized and combated self-doubt through understanding our identity, anchoring our worth in Christ, meditating on God's promises, and allowing His Word to shape our thoughts and beliefs, we are now equipped to step out in faith. This final step in overcoming self-doubt involves embracing our true potential in Christ and stepping into the purpose for which He has called us.

Stepping Out in Faith

Stepping out in faith can often feel intimidating, especially when self-doubt seeks to hold us back. However, the Bible encourages us to trust in God and lean not on our own understanding (Proverbs 3:5, ESV). Trusting in God requires a step of faith, a willingness to move forward even when the path may not be fully clear or the outcome certain.

An excellent biblical example of stepping out in faith is seen in the life of Abraham. God called him to leave his country and go to a land that He would show him (Genesis 12:1, ASV). Despite not knowing where he was going, Abraham stepped out in faith, trusting God's promise of blessing. In the same way, we are called to step out, trusting in God's promises and direction for our lives.

Embracing Our True Potential in Christ

Stepping out in faith is also about embracing our true potential in Christ. This potential is not based on our abilities, accomplishments, or the approval of others. Instead, it's anchored in our identity in Christ and the work He has accomplished on our behalf.

Paul reminds us in Philippians 4:13 (ESV) that "I can do all things through him who strengthens me." The "all things" does not imply we can accomplish anything we set our minds to, rather it means that we can endure all things through the strength provided by Christ. Our true potential is realized when we abide in Christ and rely on His strength, not our own.

Moreover, in 2 Corinthians 5:17 (ESV), we read, "Therefore, if anyone is in Christ, he is a new creation. The old has passed away; behold, the new has come." As new creations, we are not bound by our past failures, fears, or doubts. We have been given a new identity and a new life in Christ, equipping us to walk in the good works that God has prepared for us (Ephesians 2:10, ESV).

Conclusion

Overcoming self-doubt and embracing our true potential in Christ is not a one-time event, but a lifelong journey. It requires daily surrender, continuous reliance on God's Word, persistent prayer, and unwavering trust in His promises. It means stepping out in faith, even when it's uncomfortable or uncertain. As we trust God and take these steps of faith, we can experience the joy and fulfillment of walking in His purpose for our lives, overcoming self-doubt, and truly making a difference in the world for His glory.

Overcoming Obstacles and Embracing Victory

Conquering Fear and Insecurity through God's Promises

Fear and insecurity are some of the most potent triggers of self-doubt. They can discourage us, hold us back from pursuing our God-given potential, and even prevent us from making the difference we are called to make. However, God's promises found in the Bible provide a powerful antidote to fear and insecurity.

Understanding the Nature of Fear and Insecurity

Fear and insecurity often originate from focusing on our limitations or dwelling on negative experiences. We fear failure, rejection, uncertainty, and even success, and these fears breed insecurity. However, the Bible reminds us repeatedly not to be afraid.

Consider the prophet Jeremiah. God called him to a challenging task – to deliver a difficult message to a stubborn people (Jeremiah 1:7, ASV). Jeremiah was insecure, citing his youth as a reason he couldn't do what God had asked. But God replied, "Do not say, 'I am only a youth'; for to all to whom I send you, you shall go, and whatever I command you, you shall speak" (Jeremiah 1:7, ESV).

God's Promises as Antidotes to Fear and Insecurity

To conquer fear and insecurity, we must shift our focus from our limitations to God's unlimited power and unchanging promises. The Bible is rich with God's promises that we can lean on when we feel afraid or insecure.

Firstly, God promises His presence. In Deuteronomy 31:6 (ESV), Moses told the Israelites, "Be strong and courageous. Do not fear or be in dread of them, for it is the Lord your God who goes with you. He will not leave you or forsake you." The same promise applies to us today. God is with us, and His presence can dispel fear.

Secondly, God promises His power. Isaiah 41:10 (ESV) assures us, "Fear not, for I am with you; be not dismayed, for I am your God; I will strengthen you, I will help you, I will uphold you with my righteous right hand." When we feel weak or incapable, we can find strength in God's power.

Thirdly, God promises His love. In 1 John 4:18 (ESV), we learn that "There is no fear in love, but perfect love casts out fear." Understanding the depth of God's love for us can help us overcome fear and insecurity.

Applying God's Promises in Our Lives

Knowing these promises is not enough. We need to internalize them, meditate on them, and apply them in our lives. When we feel fear creeping in, we can replace fearful thoughts with God's promises.

In addition, we can pray and ask God to help us trust His promises. As we grow in our faith and understanding of God's Word, we can experience His peace, "which surpasses all understanding, will guard your hearts and your minds in Christ Jesus" (Philippians 4:7, ESV).

Conclusion

Conquering fear and insecurity is a crucial step in overcoming self-doubt and embracing our potential in Christ. It requires faith, trust in God's promises, and the courage to step out even when we feel afraid. God's promises provide us with a firm foundation on which we can stand and fight the battles of fear and insecurity. As we hold onto these promises and allow them to shape our thoughts and beliefs, we can rise above fear and insecurity, step into our God-given potential, and make a significant difference in the world.

Resting in His Strength and Finding Confidence in His Faithfulness

Overcoming self-doubt is not a task we accomplish alone. It is not about muscling our way through or attempting to muster up our strength. Instead, it involves leaning on God's strength and finding confidence in His faithfulness. God's promises are the source of our strength and the foundation of our confidence.

Understanding the Strength of God

The Bible portrays God as the source of strength for His people. It assures us that we can rely on His strength, especially when we feel weak and overwhelmed by self-doubt.

God's strength is evident in His creation. Psalm 19:1 (ASV) declares, "The heavens declare the glory of God; and the firmament showeth his handiwork." When we observe the vastness of the universe or the intricate details of nature, we witness the strength of God.

Moreover, His strength is most profoundly demonstrated in the resurrection of Jesus Christ. Ephesians 1:19-20 (ESV) says, "and what is the immeasurable greatness of his power toward us who believe, according to the working of his great might that he worked in Christ when he raised him from the dead and seated him at his right hand in the heavenly places." If God can raise Jesus from the dead, He can undoubtedly help us overcome self-doubt.

Finding Confidence in God's Faithfulness

Another essential aspect of overcoming self-doubt is finding confidence in God's faithfulness. In Lamentations 3:22-23 (ESV), we read, "The steadfast love of the LORD never ceases; his mercies never come to an end; they are new every morning; great is your faithfulness."

The faithfulness of God means that He is trustworthy and dependable. He keeps His promises, and He will not leave us or forsake us. This understanding of God's faithfulness can bolster our confidence, especially when self-doubt tries to undermine our faith.

Resting in His Strength and Faithfulness

Once we understand God's strength and faithfulness, we can rest in these truths. This rest does not imply inactivity but rather a calm reliance on God, even in the midst of our battles against self-doubt.

To rest in God's strength, we must surrender our attempts to overcome self-doubt on our own. We must acknowledge our weakness and depend on His strength. As 2 Corinthians 12:9 (ESV) reminds us, "But he said to me, 'My grace is sufficient for you, for my power is made perfect in weakness.' Therefore I will boast all the more gladly of my weaknesses, so that the power of Christ may rest upon me."

To find confidence in God's faithfulness, we must recall His past faithfulness and trust His future faithfulness. We can keep a record of the times when God has been faithful to us and remind ourselves of these instances when we feel doubtful.

Conclusion

Resting in God's strength and finding confidence in His faithfulness is key to overcoming self-doubt and embracing our potential in Christ. As we acknowledge our weakness, lean on God's strength, and trust in His faithfulness, we can overcome self-doubt. This shift in reliance allows us to step into the fullness of our potential and make a difference in the world for the glory of God.

Living Out Your God-Given Potential

Applying God's Promises in Practical Ways to Fulfill Your Purpose

Overcoming self-doubt not only requires understanding and trusting in God's promises but also entails practically applying them in our daily lives to fulfill our God-given purpose. Below, we explore some practical ways to apply God's promises to address self-doubt and live out our purpose.

Diligently Study God's Word

The first step is to make the studying and understanding of God's word a part of your daily routine. The Bible is filled with God's promises, and understanding these promises is essential to combat self-doubt. Psalm 119:105 (ASV) says, "Thy word is a lamp unto my feet, and light unto my path." The more we understand His word, the more we understand His promises and His purpose for our lives.

Memorize and Meditate on God's Promises

A practical way to apply God's promises is to memorize them. Having His promises at the forefront of our minds allows us to recall them when self-doubt begins to creep in. Joshua 1:8 (ESV) advises us, "This Book of the Law shall not depart from your mouth, but you shall meditate on it day and night, so that you may be careful to do according to all that is written in it. For then you will make your way prosperous, and then you will have good success." Meditation is more than mere recollection; it is the process of deeply thinking about God's promises, understanding them, and considering how to apply them.

Align Your Thoughts with God's Promises

Proactively aligning our thoughts with God's promises is a practical way of applying them in our lives. When thoughts of self-doubt arise, we should compare them with God's promises. If they don't align, we replace those doubts with God's truth. This practice is reflected in 2 Corinthians 10:5 (ESV), where we are encouraged to "take every thought captive to obey Christ."

Pray Using God's Promises

Incorporate God's promises in your prayers. When praying about situations causing you to doubt, remind God of His promises. This is not because He forgets but to reinforce your trust in His promises. It is also a way to align our desires with God's will as outlined in His promises.

Act on God's Promises

Applying God's promises ultimately means acting on them. This action could mean stepping out in faith, even when we feel self-doubt. God's promises are not just to be read and memorized; they are to be acted upon. James 1:22 (ESV) cautions, "But be doers of the word, and not hearers only, deceiving yourselves." By living out God's promises, we not only combat self-doubt but we also live in the fullness of God's purpose for us.

Conclusion

Overcoming self-doubt and fulfilling our purpose is not a one-time event; it is a continuous process of learning, trusting, and applying God's promises in our lives. It requires diligence, patience, and courage. As we faithfully apply these practical steps, we will find our confidence in God growing, our self-doubt diminishing, and our lives increasingly aligned with the purposes God has for us. It is in living out these promises that we truly make a difference, fulfilling our unique, God-given purpose.

Using Your Unique Gifts and Talents to Make a Difference in the World

While understanding and applying God's promises are integral in overcoming self-doubt, recognizing and utilizing our unique gifts and talents for God's glory is equally important. We each have a distinct blend of abilities, given to us by God for a specific purpose. This section explores how we can leverage these unique talents to make a difference in the world.

Understanding Your Gifts

The first step to using your gifts is understanding what they are. This understanding is often achieved through self-discovery, prayer, and sometimes through affirmation from others. According to 1 Corinthians 12:4-7 (ESV), "Now there are varieties of gifts, but the same Spirit; and there are varieties of service, but the same Lord; and there are varieties of activities, but it is the same God who empowers them all in everyone. To each is given the manifestation of the Spirit for the common good." Each of us has been given gifts by God, and these gifts are designed for service to others.

Cultivating Your Gifts

Once you've discovered your unique gifts, it's crucial to cultivate them. This means working on them, refining them, and improving your skills. In the parable of the talents (Matthew 25:14-30 ESV), Jesus commended the servants who used and multiplied their talents and rebuked the one who hid his talent. This parable teaches us the importance of making good use of the gifts God has given us.

Using Your Gifts to Serve Others

God has given us our talents and abilities, not for our own personal gain or fame but for serving others and glorifying Him. As Peter writes in 1 Peter 4:10 (ESV), "As each has received a gift, use it to serve one another, as good stewards of God's varied grace." When we use our unique abilities to serve others, we're not just making a difference in their lives; we're also fulfilling our God-given purpose.

Combating Self-Doubt with Your Gifts

God didn't give us a spirit of self-doubt or fear but of power, love, and self-discipline (2 Timothy 1:7 ESV). One of the ways we can combat self-doubt is by actively using our gifts. As we see the positive impact we can make on the world with our unique talents, it reinforces the truth of God's promises and helps diminish feelings of self-doubt.

Conclusion

God has bestowed each of us with unique gifts and talents, given out of His abundant love and grace. As we discover and cultivate these gifts, using them to serve others and make a difference in the world, we fulfill our God-given purpose and combat self-doubt. In this, we don't just affirm our worth and purpose; we also bear witness to God's incredible faithfulness and His promises, encouraging others to do the same. Through our service, we become living testimonies to God's love, making a difference in the world one act at a time.

APPENDIX D Overcoming Comparison and Embracing Your Unique Journey

Recognizing the Trap of Comparison

Understanding the Negative Impact of Comparison on Our Well-being

"Comparison is the thief of joy," so the saying goes, and it couldn't be more accurate. When we constantly compare our lives, our achievements, our looks, or our spiritual journey to others, it can be detrimental to our well-being. This section explores the negative impact of comparison and how embracing our unique journey can help mitigate this harm.

The Allure of Comparison

In today's digital age, comparison has become an almost inescapable part of our daily lives. We scroll through social media feeds that are filled with idealized, edited snapshots of people's lives, causing us to compare ourselves with these perceived perfections. The Apostle Paul, however, reminds us in 2 Corinthians 10:12 (ESV), "But when they measure themselves by one another and compare themselves with one another, they are without understanding." It's crucial to remember that these curated images are not an accurate reflection of reality.

The Negative Impact

Comparison often leads to discontentment and unhappiness. It fosters a mindset of scarcity, where we always feel like we're lacking something that others have. It can breed jealousy, envy, and low self-esteem, robbing us of the joy and contentment that God wants for us.

Proverbs 14:30 (ASV) explains, "A tranquil heart gives life to the flesh, but envy makes the bones rot."

Additionally, comparison can distort our perspective of our self-worth and value. When we base our value on how we stack up against others, it's a losing battle, because there will always be someone who appears to be doing better in some aspect of life.

Impact on Our Spiritual Lives

Comparison doesn't just affect our mental and emotional well-being; it can also have a detrimental impact on our spiritual lives. It can lead us to question God's fairness, forgetting that each of us has a unique relationship with Him and a unique purpose to fulfill. In the parable of the workers in the vineyard (Matthew 20:1-16 ESV), Jesus taught that God's generosity isn't something to be compared but to be grateful for, regardless of what He gives to others.

Embracing Our Unique Journey

Recognizing the negative impact of comparison is the first step to overcoming it. But it's equally important to embrace our unique journey in Christ. God has a different plan for each of us, tailored according to His purpose for our lives. Instead of comparing, we should focus on fulfilling the unique purpose God has for us. As the Apostle Paul reminds us in Galatians 6:4 (ESV), "But let each one test his own work, and then his reason to boast will be in himself alone and not in his neighbor."

In the end, understanding the negative impacts of comparison can help us consciously steer clear of this detrimental habit. By embracing our unique journey, we can cultivate a more fulfilling and content relationship with God and with ourselves.

Identifying the Sources and Triggers of Comparison in Our Lives

Comparison can often be a subconscious activity that seeps into our lives, pulling our focus away from our unique journey and fostering feelings of inadequacy and discontentment. To overcome comparison, we must first identify its sources and triggers in our lives. This section explores various sources and triggers of comparison, and provides guidance on how to become more aware of them.

Societal and Cultural Norms

Our society and culture can often set implicit standards that we feel compelled to live up to. These could be about appearance, career success, material possessions, or even how we practice our faith. Such standards can be a significant source of comparison, subtly making us feel inadequate or less than others. Remember, as followers of Christ, our identity and value are defined by God's love for us, not by societal or cultural norms. Romans 12:2 (ESV) urges us not to conform to the pattern of this world, but to renew our minds, so we can discern God's will.

Social Media and Technology

With the advent of social media and technology, we have more access than ever to people's lives worldwide. While this connectedness can be a source of inspiration and learning, it can also breed comparison. We often see highlight reels of people's lives, making it easy to compare and feel less than. However, these platforms seldom show the whole picture of a person's life. Proverbs 14:30 (ASV) cautions that "envy is rottenness to the bones."

Family and Peer Pressure

Family and peers can also be sources of comparison. Pressure to achieve similar successes as siblings, relatives, or peers can trigger feelings of inadequacy. Nevertheless, each of us has a unique path and timeline in life. The Parable of the Prodigal Son in Luke 15:11-32 (ESV) illustrates this as the older brother struggles with feelings of comparison and resentment, missing the broader picture of his father's love and abundance.

Personal Insecurity and Self-Doubt

Our insecurities and self-doubt can often be the most potent triggers of comparison. When we're insecure about certain aspects of our lives, we tend to look at others who excel in those areas and feel inadequate. These feelings can stem from past experiences or perceived failures. However, 2 Corinthians 12:9-10 (ESV) reassures us that in our weakness, God's power is made perfect. We don't need to compare ourselves because God's grace is sufficient for us.

Identifying the sources and triggers of comparison in our lives is a vital step in overcoming comparison. When we understand where these feelings stem from, we can be more intentional about addressing them, allowing us to fully embrace our unique journey with God.

Embracing Your Uniqueness in God's Design

Discovering the Beauty and Purpose of Your Individual Journey

The journey of faith is a personal one, unique to each of us. While it can be easy to fall into the trap of comparison, it's essential to realize that each individual's journey has its beauty and purpose. This section seeks to enlighten us on the importance of discovering and cherishing our individual journey with God.

Recognizing the Uniqueness of Your Journey

First, we must understand that each of us has a unique journey with God. Psalm 139:13-16 (ESV) tells us that God knit us together in our mother's womb, and all our days were written in His book before any of them came to be. Each of us was created with a purpose in God's plan, with a unique set of experiences, gifts, and circumstances. While the world and even other Christians might try to define success in certain ways, God's definition of success is to be faithful to Him and to follow the path He has laid out for us.

Appreciating the Beauty of Your Journey

As we acknowledge the uniqueness of our journey, we should also learn to appreciate its beauty. Even our struggles and trials have a purpose. James 1:2-4 (ASV) tells us to count it all joy when we fall into various trials, knowing that the testing of our faith produces endurance, and that endurance has its perfect work, that we may be perfect and entire, lacking in nothing. Our trials shape us, molding us into the people God wants us to be and equipping us for the work He has prepared for us.

Seeking God's Purpose in Your Journey

Discovering God's purpose in our journey involves continuous communication with Him through prayer and reading His Word. Jeremiah 29:11 (ESV) assures us that God has plans for us, plans for welfare and not for evil, to give us a future and a hope. By staying in tune with God and seeking His will, we can discern His purpose for our journey.

Staying Focused on Your Journey

In Philippians 3:13-14 (ASV), the Apostle Paul talks about forgetting what lies behind and reaching forward to what lies ahead, pressing on toward the goal for the prize of the high calling of God in Christ Jesus. This should be our attitude as well - focusing on our journey, rather than comparing it with others.

Understanding that God has a unique purpose for each of us and focusing on that instead of comparing our journey to others is a liberating and fulfilling way to live our Christian life. As we each run our race, let's remember to encourage one another, appreciating the unique beauty and purpose of each journey.

Recognizing God's Intentional Design and Plan for Your Life

The battle against comparison requires a deep understanding and appreciation of God's individual, intentional design and plan for our lives. We each have a unique path, crafted with purpose by the divine Creator. Embracing this truth can free us from the shackles of comparison and allow us to live out our God-given purpose with authenticity and joy.

God's Intentional Design

The idea that God has intentionally designed each one of us is not a novel concept. It is a truth firmly rooted in the Scriptures. Psalm 139:13-14 (ESV) confirms this, saying, "For you formed my inward parts; you knitted me together in my mother's womb. I praise you, for

I am fearfully and wonderfully made. Wonderful are your works; my soul knows it very well."

God's craftsmanship is exquisite, unique, and intentional. Our physical attributes, personality traits, talents, and abilities were all crafted by God's hand. In other words, God has given us our individuality for a reason. It's part of His perfect design.

God's Plan for Your Life

In addition to designing us intentionally, God also has a unique plan for each of our lives. Jeremiah 29:11 (ESV) reassures us of this, saying, "For I know the plans I have for you, declares the Lord, plans for welfare and not for evil, to give you a future and a hope."

God has ordained a specific path for each one of us to walk. This path is not random or haphazard; it is designed with our welfare in mind and intended to fulfill His purposes.

Accepting God's Design and Plan

Accepting God's design and plan for our lives involves a deliberate decision to trust Him and to reject the compulsion to compare ourselves with others. Proverbs 3:5-6 (ASV) encourages us to, "Trust in the Lord with all your heart, And lean not upon your own understanding: In all thy ways acknowledge Him, And He will direct your paths."

By trusting in God's design and plan for our lives, we can overcome the temptation to compare ourselves to others and instead focus on walking the unique path God has set before us.

Living Out God's Design and Plan

Once we've recognized and accepted God's intentional design and plan for our lives, it's time to live it out. Ephesians 2:10 (ESV) tells us that we are "His workmanship, created in Christ Jesus for good works, which God prepared beforehand, that we should walk in them."

We must actively seek to live out God's plan and use the unique design He has given us to accomplish the good works He has prepared for us. This means embracing our individuality, using our talents and gifts for His glory, and pursuing the purposes He has set for our lives.

In conclusion, recognizing and accepting God's intentional design and plan for our lives is key to overcoming comparison. When we embrace our uniqueness and pursue God's individual plan for us, we can find true fulfillment and make a real difference in the world for His glory.

Shifting Your Focus to God's Approval

Breaking Free from the Need for Validation from Others

The desire for approval and acceptance is a universal human need. However, when our need for validation from others dictates our self-worth and guides our actions, it can be detrimental to our spiritual and emotional well-being. A fundamental aspect of overcoming comparison and embracing our unique journey is learning to break free from the need for external validation.

The Danger of Seeking Validation from Others

Seeking validation from others can lead us into a trap of perpetual dissatisfaction and insecurity. The Bible warns against this in Proverbs 29:25 (ESV), stating, "The fear of man lays a snare, but whoever trusts in the Lord is safe." The 'fear of man' here can also be understood as the overwhelming desire to please others and to seek their approval. When we allow the opinions of others to define our worth and dictate our actions, we essentially become enslaved to their views, leading us away from the path God has laid out for us.

The Source of True Validation

Our value and worth should not be determined by the validation of others but by the One who created us. In Isaiah 43:4 (ASV), God declares, "Since you were precious in my sight, you have been honorable, and I have loved you." The ultimate validation comes from God, who sees us as precious, honors us, and loves us unconditionally. This divine validation is steady and unchanging, unlike human validation which can be fickle and fleeting.

Breaking Free through Faith and Assurance in God

To break free from the need for external validation, we need to have faith and find our assurance in God. Galatians 1:10 (ESV) states, "For am I now seeking the approval of man, or of God? Or am I trying to please man? If I were still trying to please man, I would not be a servant of Christ." The Apostle Paul makes it clear that seeking validation from man hinders our service to Christ. Instead, we are called to seek approval from God, and to find our worth and identity in Him.

Living for God, Not for Approval

Once we break free from the need for external validation, we can live our lives fully for God, according to His design and plan. As stated in Colossians 3:23-24 (ESV), "Whatever you do, work heartily, as for the Lord and not for men, knowing that from the Lord you will receive the inheritance as your reward. You are serving the Lord Christ." By focusing on God's approval and not that of man, we are released from the burden of trying to measure up to others' expectations, and can experience freedom, peace, and the joy of serving Christ.

In conclusion, breaking free from the need for external validation is a crucial step in overcoming comparison and embracing our unique journey. By recognizing that our true worth comes from God and not from others, we can live out God's design and plan for our lives with confidence and authenticity.

Finding Security and Fulfillment in God's Unconditional Love and Acceptance

In our journey to overcome comparison and embrace our unique path, a key cornerstone is understanding and resting in God's unconditional love and acceptance. This divine love provides the secure foundation on which we can build our lives, helping us find lasting fulfillment that is independent of others' opinions or the world's shifting standards.

The Reality of God's Unconditional Love

God's love for us is clear, steadfast, and does not hinge on our performance, achievements, or the approval of others. Romans 5:8 (ESV) communicates this truth powerfully, "but God shows his love for us in that while we were still sinners, Christ died for us." This is the ultimate demonstration of unconditional love. While we were estranged from God because of sin, He offered the precious gift of His Son. His love doesn't fluctuate based on our failings or successes—it remains constant.

Security in God's Love

Our security should not be tied to the fleeting things of this world but anchored in God's unchanging love. When we find our security in God's love, it creates a buffer against the waves of comparison, insecurity, and self-doubt. The Psalmist captures this sentiment in Psalms 62:2 (ASV), "He only is my rock and my salvation, my fortress. I shall not be greatly shaken." With God as our rock, we can withstand the pressures and temptations to conform or compare ourselves with others.

Fulfillment in God's Love

True fulfillment is not found in human validation but in the love and acceptance of our heavenly Father. In the depth of His love, we find our value, purpose, and satisfaction. Jeremiah 31:3 (ESV) conveys this, "I have loved you with an everlasting love; therefore I have continued my faithfulness to you." This everlasting love is a source of fulfillment that won't run dry, unlike worldly pleasures or human praise that can be inconsistent and momentary.

Experiencing God's Unconditional Love

To experience God's unconditional love, we need to have a personal relationship with Jesus Christ. As stated in John 3:16 (ESV), "For God so loved the world, that he gave his only Son, that whoever believes in him should not perish but have eternal life." This loving relationship is open to all who believe in Christ, leading to eternal life and access to God's unending love.

In overcoming comparison and embracing our unique journey, understanding, and accepting God's unconditional love is pivotal. This love reassures us of our worth, provides security amidst life's uncertainties, and grants us fulfillment that surpasses all worldly measures. As we move forward in our unique journeys, let us anchor ourselves in God's unfailing love, finding therein our ultimate security and fulfillment. In doing so, we can truly make a difference in the world as unique individuals, secure and complete in God's love.

However: The Necessary Clarification of God's 'Unconditional' Love and Acceptance

However, it is essential to note that the term "unconditional love" does not imply that God's love permits or condones all actions, or that there are no consequences for sin. The concept of God's "unconditional love" often misconstrued, requires us to look closer into the biblical understanding of God's love and His righteousness.

God's Love and His Righteousness

The Bible clearly communicates that God is love (1 John 4:8, ESV) and at the same time, He is perfectly holy and just (Revelation 4:8, ASV). He does not compromise His righteousness because of His love. His love led Him to provide a way of salvation through Jesus Christ (John 3:16, ESV), but He does not ignore or trivialize sin. His unconditional love doesn't excuse sin; it offers redemption from it.

Conditional Aspects in Relationship with God

It's true that certain aspects of our relationship with God are conditional. In John 15:10 (ESV), Jesus says, "If you keep my commandments, you will abide in my love, just as I have kept my Father's commandments and abide in his love." Here, abiding in Christ's love is linked to the condition of obedience to His commands. God's love remains constant, but our experience of His love and blessings is influenced by our response to Him.

The Misunderstanding of 'Unconditional Love'

Unfortunately, the phrase "unconditional love" can be misleading if not properly understood. It is not an open invitation to continue in sin without consequences. Romans 6:1-2 (ESV) raises and answers this wrong idea, "What shall we say then? Are we to continue in sin that grace may abound? By no means! How can we who died to sin still live in it?" God's grace and love are not a license to sin, but a motivation for us to repent and live righteously.

Conclusion: A Balanced View of God's Love

In conclusion, it is crucial to hold a balanced view of God's love. Yes, God's love is vast and relentless, reaching out to us even in our sinfulness. Yet, it is not a lenient acceptance of all our actions, regardless of their alignment with His holy nature and righteous laws. In embracing our unique journey, we must respond to God's love by obeying His commandments, rejecting sin, and pursuing righteousness. This way, we truly align ourselves with His divine will and purpose.

Cultivating Gratitude and Contentment

Practicing Gratitude to Combat the Tendency to Compare

Comparison can lead to self-deprecation, envy, or pride, thereby destabilizing the Christian journey. It deviates focus from the divine assignment God has for each individual and creates a toxic cycle of unfulfillment and discontent. Gratitude, however, is a potent antidote to the disease of comparison. When we consciously practice gratitude, we shift our focus from what we lack to the abundance we already possess. This simple act of acknowledging and appreciating God's gifts in our lives can profoundly transform our perspective and empower us to embrace our unique journey.

Understanding Gratitude from a Biblical Perspective

Gratitude is a recurring theme in the scriptures. "Give thanks in all circumstances; for this is the will of God in Christ Jesus for you," 1 Thessalonians 5:18 (ESV) says. This verse doesn't suggest we should be thankful for all circumstances, including the painful or difficult ones, but rather in them. Despite the trials we encounter, God's presence and His love remain constant. For these, we can always be grateful.

The Power of Gratitude in Fostering Contentment

Gratitude encourages contentment by helping us see the value in what we have rather than longing for what we don't. It aligns with the apostle Paul's words in Philippians 4:11-12 (ESV), "Not that I am speaking of being in need, for I have learned in whatever situation I am to be content. I know how to be brought low, and I know how to abound. In any and every circumstance, I have learned the secret of facing plenty and hunger, abundance and need."

Gratitude Refocuses our Perception

Comparison makes us perceive our blessings as never enough because there is always someone who has more or better. On the other hand, gratitude reverses this perception, making us see our lives as overflowing with blessings. Psalm 23:5 (ASV) says, "Thou preparest a table before me in the presence of mine enemies: Thou hast anointed my head with oil; My cup runneth over." The psalmist's recognition of God's abundant provision in his life refocuses his perception from his enemies to God's blessings, and this shift in focus is made possible through gratitude.

Gratitude Encourages Humility

Gratitude acknowledges that all we have and are is by God's grace, not merely by our merit. As stated in James 1:17 (ESV), "Every good gift and every perfect gift is from above, coming down from the Father of lights with whom there is no variation or shadow due to change." Recognizing God as the source of all our blessings fosters humility and discourages prideful comparisons.

Practicing Gratitude: Practical Steps

Practicing gratitude can be done in various ways, such as maintaining a gratitude journal, expressing thanks in prayers, or verbally acknowledging our blessings to others. Regularly practicing gratitude will not only combat the tendency to compare but also deepen our relationship with God as we continually acknowledge His love and providence in our lives.

Conclusion: Gratitude, the Antidote to Comparison

In conclusion, gratitude is more than just saying "thank you." It's a transformative practice that shifts our focus from ourselves and our perceived inadequacies to God and His abundant blessings. It is the key to overcoming comparison and embracing our unique journey with joy and contentment. As we consciously and consistently practice gratitude, we can resist the lure of comparison and grow in our understanding of God's personal love and unique plan for our lives.

Finding Contentment in God's Provision and Blessings for Your Own Journey

As Christians, the pursuit of contentment should not be a struggle against our circumstances, but a cultivation of the ability to rest in God's goodness and care. This restfulness and tranquility of spirit come not from the abundance of our possessions or the fulfillment of our earthly ambitions, but from understanding and accepting God's provisions and blessings for our personal journey. This perception allows us to overcome the inclination to compare ourselves with others and instead appreciate our unique path in life.

The Biblical Perspective on Contentment

The Bible instructs us to find contentment in God's provision. Hebrews 13:5 (ESV) says, "Keep your life free from love of money, and be content with what you have, for he has said, 'I will never leave you nor forsake you.'" Money and material possessions are temporary and cannot provide lasting happiness or security. True contentment comes from acknowledging God's continual presence and provision in our lives.

God's Provision is Enough

God provides for our needs according to His riches and wisdom. In the Old Testament, when the Israelites were wandering in the desert, God provided them with manna from heaven. Exodus 16:18 (ASV) says, "And when they measured it with an omer, he that gathered much had nothing over, and he that gathered little had no lack." This event teaches us that God's provision is enough and customized to meet our personal needs. We must, therefore, not compare our blessings with those of others.

Understanding God's Blessings

It's important to understand that God's blessings are not only material but also spiritual and eternal. Ephesians 1:3 (ESV) says, "Blessed be the God and Father of our Lord Jesus Christ, who has blessed us in Christ with every spiritual blessing in the heavenly places." Often, we overlook these spiritual blessings in our pursuit of material gain. We need to shift our focus and start appreciating these eternal blessings.

Finding Contentment in God's Blessings

The apostle Paul spoke about learning to be content in every circumstance, whether in plenty or in want (Philippians 4:11-13, ESV). This state of mind is achieved not through mere human effort but through Christ who strengthens us. Realizing this truth, we should focus on being grateful for God's blessings, both big and small, and trust in His promises.

Cultivating Contentment: Practical Steps

1. **Regular prayer and meditation on God's word:** These practices help us build a deeper relationship with God, understand His promises, and acknowledge His work in our lives.//
2. **Adopting a lifestyle of simplicity:** The less we are attached to material things, the more we can appreciate the richness of God's blessings.
3. **Gratitude:** As previously discussed, gratitude shifts our focus from what we lack to what we already have. It helps us appreciate God's blessings and fosters contentment.
4. **Trust in God's promises:** God has promised to meet our needs (Matthew 6:31-33, ESV). Trusting in His provision encourages contentment.

Conclusion: Embracing Contentment in God's Provision

In conclusion, contentment in God's provision is key to overcoming comparison and embracing our unique journey. It's about understanding and appreciating God's blessings, realizing His sufficiency, and cultivating a heart of gratitude. As we actively pursue contentment in God's provision, we can truly experience the peace and joy that comes from knowing we are secure in His loving hands. God has a unique journey for each of us, and it's time we find contentment in our own path, empowered by His unending grace and provisions.

Celebrating Others without Comparison

Learning to Genuinely Rejoice in the Success and Blessings of Others

A significant step towards overcoming comparison and embracing our unique journey in Christ is learning to genuinely rejoice in the success and blessings of others. This not only fosters a sense of unity and community within the body of Christ but also cultivates a spirit of contentment and gratitude in our hearts. Rejoicing in others' victories and blessings means understanding and accepting that God's blessings are not a zero-sum game, but rather an expression of His abundant love and grace.

Biblical Foundations for Rejoicing with Others

The Bible gives us clear instructions about sharing joy with our brothers and sisters. In Romans 12:15 (ESV), we read, "Rejoice with those who rejoice, weep with those who weep." This verse emphasizes the importance of empathy, of sharing in the experiences of others, whether they are of joy or sorrow.

Overcoming the Barrier of Envy

Often, the obstacle that prevents us from genuinely rejoicing in other people's blessings and achievements is envy. Envy is a destructive emotion that can lead to discontentment, bitterness, and resentment. James 3:16 (ESV) warns, "For where jealousy and selfish ambition exist, there will be disorder and every vile practice." To overcome envy, we must turn our eyes upon Jesus, understanding that He has a unique plan for each of us.

Finding Joy in God's Sovereignty

Believing in God's sovereignty and justice helps us rejoice in the success of others. In Matthew 20:1-16, Jesus tells the parable of the workers in the vineyard. The workers who started early in the morning were paid the same as those who started late in the day. Initially, the workers who started early grumbled because they thought they deserved more. However, the master of the vineyard, symbolizing God, reminded them of His right to do what He wants with what belongs to Him.

In the same way, God's blessings to others should not make us feel as if we have been shortchanged. Instead, it should lead us to rejoice, knowing that God is generous and fair. We should learn to trust in His wisdom and timing and find joy in His goodness to others.

Cultivating a Heart of Rejoicing: Practical Steps

1. **Prayer:** Pray for a heart that genuinely rejoices in the success and blessings of others. Ask God to remove any hint of envy or bitterness.

2. **Celebrate with others:** Take active steps to celebrate other people's victories. This can be as simple as a congratulatory message or as elaborate as organizing a celebration for them.

3. **Practice gratitude:** Cultivate a habit of thanking God for His blessings in your life and in the lives of others.

4. **Study God's Word:** Understanding God's character and His promises helps us rejoice in His goodness to others.

Conclusion: A Journey of Joy

Learning to genuinely rejoice in the success and blessings of others is a journey, one that can significantly transform our relationships and our walk with Christ. As we strive to embrace this mindset, we affirm that every blessing comes from our generous and loving Father. As we learn to celebrate with others in their moments of joy, we find ourselves growing in contentment, gratitude, and love, qualities that beautifully reflect the heart of Christ.

This journey is not just about personal growth; it's about glorifying God by loving and rejoicing with His people. So, let's begin this journey today, fully aware of God's unique plan for each of us, and commit to genuinely rejoice in the success and blessings of our brothers and sisters in Christ.

Cultivating a Spirit of Love, Support, and Encouragement within Community

In the journey towards overcoming comparison and embracing your unique journey in Christ, one indispensable element is fostering a spirit of love, support, and encouragement within your community. As members of the body of Christ, we are called to uplift and edify one another, not compete against each other. The spirit of unity, love, and mutual edification can profoundly change our perspective, helping us view our brothers and sisters not as rivals, but as fellow pilgrims in the journey of faith.

The Biblical Imperative of Love and Support

The Bible provides clear instructions about the importance of love, support, and encouragement within the Christian community. The apostle Paul, in his first letter to the Thessalonians, exhorted, "Therefore encourage one another and build each other up, just as in fact you are doing" (1 Thessalonians 5:11, ESV). The Greek word for encouragement used here is 'parakaleo,' meaning to call near, to comfort, to urge.

In another instance, the book of Hebrews reminds us, "And let us consider how to stir up one another to love and good works" (Hebrews 10:24, ESV). The word 'stir up' in Greek is 'paroxysmos,' which means to incite or stimulate. This suggests that we should not passively wait for opportunities but actively seek ways to promote love and good works among our brethren.

Love as a Reflection of God's Character

Love is the foundational virtue of the Christian faith, reflecting the very character of God. Jesus proclaimed, "A new command I give you: Love one another. As I have loved you, so you must love one another" (John 13:34, ESV). Loving one another in our community isn't optional; it is a clear command from Christ Himself. Such love should be marked by sacrificial giving, understanding, patience, and kindness.

Support in Times of Need

Providing support to our brothers and sisters in times of need is another essential aspect of Christian community. Galatians 6:2 (ESV) reminds us, "Bear one another's burdens, and so fulfill the law of Christ." Helping each other, both physically and spiritually, not only demonstrates Christ's love but also strengthens our communal bonds.

Cultivating a Spirit of Encouragement

1. **Prayer:** Pray for the well-being of others and ask God to guide you in how to support and encourage them.
2. **Positive Words:** Use your words to uplift and edify others. An encouraging word can have a powerful impact on a person's day and even their life.
3. **Active Listening:** Show empathy by actively listening to the concerns of your brothers and sisters.
4. **Service:** Serve others in love. Small acts of service can go a long way in showing your support.
5. **Forgiveness:** Practice forgiveness as a way of demonstrating love and maintaining unity within your community.

Conclusion: Building a Supportive and Loving Community

As we endeavor to overcome comparison and embrace our unique journey in Christ, let's cultivate a community characterized by love, support, and encouragement. When we begin to view others not as rivals but as companions in our faith journey, we can grow together towards maturity in Christ.

Through prayer, positive words, active listening, service, and forgiveness, we can create an environment where every member feels valued, loved, and encouraged. Remember, "By this all people will know that you are my disciples, if you have love for one another" (John 13:35, ESV). Let's strive to be a community where God's love is so evident that it points others towards Him.

Finding Your True Identity in Christ

Anchoring Your Identity in God's Truth and Not in Comparison

Comparison can be a dangerous trap. It can make us insecure, envious, and discontent. Instead of reveling in God's unique gifts and callings in our lives, we may end up coveting what others have. To overcome this, it's vital to anchor our identity not in the shifting sands of comparison, but in the solid rock of God's truth about us. This section will help illuminate how to do this, using key scriptural insights.

The Danger of Comparison

In comparing ourselves with others, we unknowingly invite discontent and dissatisfaction into our hearts. The Apostle Paul cautioned, "But when they measure themselves by one another and compare themselves with one another, they are without understanding" (2 Corinthians 10:12, ESV). The danger lies in measuring our worth by worldly standards instead of God's. It's a misunderstanding of what our identity truly is.

Your True Identity in Christ

First and foremost, our identity is rooted in our relationship with Christ. Paul states, "Therefore, if anyone is in Christ, he is a new creation. The old has passed away; behold, the new has come" (2 Corinthians 5:17, ESV). Our identity is not based on our achievements, possessions, or status, but on being God's beloved children, made new in Christ.

Accepting God's Unchanging View of You

God's view of you is not swayed by your successes or failures. His love for you is unwavering, and His promise of salvation is unchanging. Isaiah affirmed this when he wrote, "Fear not, for I have redeemed you; I have called you by name, you are mine" (Isaiah 43:1, ASV). This declaration is a powerful antidote to the insidious poison of comparison.

Finding Worth in God's Truth

Anchor your identity in the truth of what God says about you. The book of Ephesians provides an illuminating list: chosen by God, redeemed, sealed with the Holy Spirit, God's workmanship, brought near by the blood of Christ, and much more (Ephesians 1-2, ESV). By focusing on these truths, you can combat feelings of inferiority and inadequacy that comparison often brings.

Living Out Your Unique Call

Every believer has a unique role in God's grand plan. "For we are his workmanship, created in Christ Jesus for good works, which God prepared beforehand, that we should walk in them" (Ephesians 2:10, ESV). Instead of comparing your path with others', seek to discern and live out God's unique call for your life.

Steps to Anchoring Your Identity in God's Truth

1. **Bible Study:** Regularly study God's word to understand and internalize what it says about you. God's truth about you is the only accurate measure of your worth.

2. **Prayer:** Pray for wisdom and understanding to see yourself as God sees you. Ask Him to help you value His perspective above all else.

3. **Reflection:** Reflect on God's truth. Write down key scriptural insights about your identity and regularly remind yourself of them.

4. **Community:** Surround yourself with fellow believers who can encourage and affirm your identity in Christ.

5. **Action:** Live out your unique call. Use your gifts and talents to serve God and others, thereby affirming your God-given identity.

Conclusion: A Firm Identity in God's Truth

Comparison distracts us from appreciating God's unique design for our lives. By anchoring our identity in God's truth rather than in comparison, we can overcome these distractions. Understanding and accepting our true identity in Christ liberates us to joyfully live out our unique callings, secure in the unchanging love and acceptance of God. Let's anchor ourselves in His truth and walk confidently in the unique path He has laid out for us.

Embracing Your Unique Gifts, Talents, and Calling in Him

Understanding and accepting our unique gifts, talents, and calling in Christ is a pivotal aspect of overcoming comparison and embracing our unique journey. God's design for each of us is intricate and unique. As we unwrap the beauty of our God-given abilities and calling, we start to see the incomparable nature of our journey. This section will explore how we can embrace our unique endowments in Him, highlighting their significance in our Christian life.

Understanding Your Unique Gifts and Talents

The Bible affirms that God has uniquely endowed each of us with certain gifts and talents. As Paul explains in 1 Corinthians 12:4-6, ESV: "Now there are varieties of gifts, but the same Spirit; and there are varieties of service, but the same Lord; and there are varieties of activities, but it is the same God who empowers them all in everyone."

God has chosen to impart different gifts and talents to each of us, not for our self-glorification, but for the edification of His body, the church. Recognizing and acknowledging these unique gifts is the first step in embracing them.

Appreciating Your God-given Calling

Every believer has a unique calling from God. This calling is not simply about what we do; rather, it reflects who we are in Him and how we are to live in the light of that reality. Paul states in Ephesians 4:1, ESV: "I therefore, a prisoner for the Lord, urge you to walk in a manner worthy of the calling to which you have been called."

Our calling might involve specific tasks or roles, but at its core, it is about embracing God's will for our lives and living in alignment with His purposes.

Embracing Your Uniqueness in Him

Understanding and acknowledging your unique gifts, talents, and calling are important, but they are not enough. You need to embrace them. This means being comfortable with who you are in Christ and recognizing that your value and worth come from Him, not from what others think or say about you.

Paul's declaration in Galatians 2:20, ESV: "I have been crucified with Christ. It is no longer I who live, but Christ who lives in me," serves as a reminder that our true identity is found in Christ, not in worldly standards or comparisons.

Walking in Your Unique Calling

Once you've embraced your unique gifts, talents, and calling, it's time to start walking in them. This involves using your abilities for God's glory and seeking to fulfill His specific purpose for your life.

The parable of the talents in Matthew 25:14-30, ESV, provides a powerful example of how we should put our gifts to work. The servants who used their talents wisely were commended by their master, while the one who hid his talent was rebuked. God wants us to use the abilities He has given us, not hide or neglect them out of fear or comparison.

Steps to Embracing Your Unique Gifts, Talents, and Calling in Him

1. **Bible Study:** Study the Scriptures to understand what they say about spiritual gifts and God's calling.
2. **Prayer:** Ask God to help you understand and embrace your unique gifts, talents, and calling.

3. **Reflection:** Reflect on your abilities and experiences. What do they tell you about your unique gifts and calling?
4. **Community:** Share your insights with other believers and seek their feedback and support.
5. **Action:** Begin to use your gifts and talents in service to God and others. Seek opportunities that align with your unique calling.

Conclusion: Embracing Your Uniqueness

Our unique gifts, talents, and calling are not reasons for pride or comparison; instead, they're evidence of God's intricate design and boundless love for us. By understanding, acknowledging, and embracing these gifts and callings, we can start to see ourselves as God sees us: unique, valuable, and called for His purposes. When we anchor our identity in these truths, the temptation to compare dwindles, and our joy and contentment in Him grow.

God has set us each on a unique journey. As we walk this path with Him, let us cherish our distinct gifts and callings, using them for His glory and the edification of His body, the church. In doing so, we truly make a difference in the world.

Living Authentically and Pursuing Purpose

Embracing Your Authentic Self and Living Out Your God-Given Purpose

Embarking on the journey of self-discovery and purpose-driven living demands courage, but the Christian journey provides us with a strong foundation. The message of Christ encourages us to embrace our authentic selves and live out our God-given purposes. This section will focus on how to harness the power of authenticity and purposeful living to overcome comparison.

Understanding Authenticity in Christ

To live authentically, we must first understand what it means to be authentic. Authenticity entails living in alignment with our true selves, which in the Christian context means living in harmony with our identity in Christ. In 2 Corinthians 5:17, ESV, the apostle Paul declares, "Therefore, if anyone is in Christ, he is a new creation. The old has passed away; behold, the new has come."

Our authenticity stems from our new nature in Christ, and it's this new self we need to embrace.

Finding and Living Out Your God-Given Purpose

As believers, we are not aimless wanderers. God has created each of us for a specific purpose. Ephesians 2:10, ESV, tells us, "For we are his workmanship, created in Christ Jesus for good works, which God prepared beforehand, that we should walk in them." Our purpose is not a burden to bear, but a gift to embrace. It is our unique contribution to the world, a way of living that reflects God's glory and furthers His kingdom.

Authentic Living in the Face of Comparison

In a world that often promotes comparison and conformity, living authentically is a powerful way to stand out and live freely. Authentic living means being true to who God created you to be, rather than striving to meet others' expectations or fit into worldly molds.

Romans 12:2, ESV, gives us clear guidance: "Do not be conformed to this world, but be transformed by the renewal of your mind, that by testing you may discern what is the will of God, what is good and acceptable and perfect." Living authentically enables us to experience freedom from comparison and the peace that comes from being in God's will.

Embracing Your Authentic Self and God-Given Purpose

Embracing your authentic self and God-given purpose requires self-awareness, courage, and faith. It means recognizing and accepting your unique strengths, weaknesses, passions, and calling, and aligning your life accordingly. The Psalmist beautifully encapsulates this concept in Psalm 139:14, ASV: "I will give thanks unto thee; for I am fearfully and wonderfully made: Wonderful are thy works; and that my soul knoweth right well."

Steps to Embrace Authenticity and Purpose

1. **Discover:** Start by discovering who you are in Christ and what His Word says about your worth and purpose.

2. **Acknowledge:** Acknowledge your unique attributes, gifts, and calling. Understand that they are God-given and for His glory.

3. **Embrace:** Embrace your authentic self and God-given purpose. Let go of the need to compare or conform.

4. **Live out:** Strive to live in alignment with your true self and God-given purpose. Reflect Christ in all you do.

Conclusion: Living Authentically and Purposefully

Living authentically and purposefully brings immense joy and fulfillment. It liberates us from the shackles of comparison and helps us embrace our God-given journey with gratitude and contentment. When we choose to embrace our authentic selves and live out our God-given purposes, we are not only honoring God but also making a meaningful difference in the world. Remember, you are "fearfully and wonderfully made" (Psalm 139:14, ASV), and God has a unique purpose for your life. Step into it with confidence and joy, knowing you are loved, valued, and purposed by the Creator of the universe.

Trusting God's Guidance and Stepping Confidently into Your Unique Journey

One of the most beautiful aspects of being a follower of Christ is the promise of God's guidance and provision in our lives. As we learn to trust Him more, we can step confidently into our unique journey, free from the fear and burden of comparison. This section will explore the importance of trust in God's guidance and how it can empower us to embrace our unique journey with confidence.

Understanding God's Guidance

Scripture is abundant with examples and promises of God's guidance. Psalm 32:8, ASV, affirms this: "I will instruct thee and teach thee in the way which thou shalt go: I will counsel thee with mine eye upon thee." This divine guidance is not abstract or distant; it is personal and intimate. When we put our trust in God, we can confidently step into our unique journey, knowing He is leading us.

Trusting God's Guidance

Trust in God's guidance requires faith and surrender. Faith, because we believe in His sovereignty and goodness, even when we don't understand His ways. Surrender, because we choose His will over our own. Proverbs 3:5-6, ESV, provides wisdom on this: "Trust in the Lord with all your heart, and do not lean on your own understanding. In all your ways acknowledge him, and he will make straight your paths."

Trusting God's guidance is not about blind faith or complacency, but rather active reliance on His promises and faithfulness.

Stepping Confidently into Your Unique Journey

Once we trust in God's guidance, we can step confidently into our unique journey. We no longer need to compare our path with others because we know that our journey is divinely ordained and directed. As the apostle Paul writes in Galatians 6:4, ESV: "But let each one test his own work, and then his reason to boast will be in himself alone and not in his neighbor."

Our unique journey may not mirror that of our peers, and that's okay. Our duty is not to duplicate another's journey but to faithfully follow the path that God has set before us.

Embracing the Journey with Confidence and Joy

Embracing our unique journey is not about striving for perfection or attaining worldly success. Instead, it is about living in faithfulness and obedience to God's will, seeking His kingdom above all else. Matthew 6:33, ASV, exhorts us to, "seek ye first his kingdom, and his righteousness; and all these things shall be added unto you."

As we trust in God's guidance and step confidently into our unique journey, we can experience peace and joy that transcends worldly standards. It frees us from the burden of comparison and enables us to celebrate the work of God in and through our lives.

Conclusion: Trusting and Stepping Confidently into God's Plan

Trusting in God's guidance and stepping confidently into your unique journey can transform your life. It is a journey that moves beyond comparison and taps into the extraordinary potential of living in alignment with God's will. It fosters a deep sense of purpose, peace, and fulfillment that the world can never offer.

Remember, our God is a personal guide and His guidance is perfect. As we learn to trust Him, we can confidently step into our unique journey and live out our God-given purpose. Our individual paths may look different, but they all lead to the same destination: a life that glorifies God and brings us ultimate joy and satisfaction. Trust Him and step confidently into your unique journey, for He "will instruct thee and teach thee in the way which thou shalt go: I will counsel thee with mine eye upon thee" (Psalm 32:8, ASV).

APPENDIX E Overcoming Self-Criticism: Embracing God's Unconditional Love

Recognizing the Power of Self-Criticism

Understanding the Negative Impact of Self-Criticism on Our Well-Being

The human mind, gifted with intelligence and consciousness, also possesses a characteristic of introspection. This enables us to reflect on our actions and decisions, thereby learning and growing. However, when self-reflection turns into self-criticism, it can impact our well-being negatively. This chapter examines the harmful effects of self-criticism and how understanding and embracing God's unconditional love can help us overcome this.

The Detrimental Nature of Self-Criticism

Self-criticism typically originates from an internal dialogue, often characterized by judgment, comparison, and dissatisfaction. While it might seem helpful or even necessary for personal growth, it often deteriorates into an unproductive and harmful cycle.

The Bible warns against such destructive behavior. In Proverbs 14:21, ASV, it says, "He that despiseth his neighbor is void of wisdom: But a man of understanding holdeth his peace." If we substitute 'self' for 'neighbor' here, it becomes apparent that despising oneself, which includes excessive self-criticism, is not an act of wisdom.

The Psychological Impact of Self-Criticism

Psychologically, self-criticism can be detrimental. It often leads to decreased self-esteem, increased anxiety, and a distorted self-image. This can manifest in a myriad of ways, from withdrawal from social situations to reluctance in taking on new challenges and even physical symptoms such as sleep disturbances or mood disorders.

The Spiritual Impact of Self-Criticism

From a spiritual perspective, self-criticism can impede our relationship with God. By constantly belittling ourselves, we can unconsciously question God's creation and His plans for us. This view is contrary to Psalm 139:14, ESV, which states, "I praise you, for I am fearfully and wonderfully made. Wonderful are your works; my soul knows it very well."

Self-Criticism vs. Constructive Self-Reflection

There is a difference between constructive self-reflection and detrimental self-criticism. Constructive self-reflection is a practice of considering one's actions and experiences with the intention of learning and growth. It is aligned with 2 Corinthians 13:5, ESV, "Examine yourselves, to see whether you are in the faith. Test yourselves. Or do you not realize this about yourselves, that Jesus Christ is in you?—unless indeed you fail to meet the test!"

On the other hand, self-criticism involves dwelling on negative aspects, often without any productive outcome. It doesn't lead to growth or improvement but to self-doubt, insecurity, and even self-loathing.

Conclusion: The Need for Embracing God's Unconditional Love

Understanding the negative impact of self-criticism on our well-being is the first step towards overcoming it. However, understanding alone is not enough. We must replace this harmful practice with the acceptance and embracement of God's unconditional love.

God's love, unlike our flawed self-criticism, is perfect and unwavering. As stated in Romans 8:38-39, ESV, "For I am sure that neither death nor life, nor angels nor rulers, nor things present nor things to come, nor powers, nor height nor depth, nor anything else in all creation, will be able to separate us from the love of God in Christ Jesus our Lord."

Replacing self-criticism with God's unconditional love can dramatically improve our well-being. Instead of judging and belittling ourselves, we can find peace, joy, and confidence in God's love. When we understand and embrace this truth, we can overcome self-criticism and live out our God-given purpose with joy and confidence.

Acknowledging the Need for Change and Embracing God's Love

The act of self-criticism, as previously discussed, is a harmful habit that has both psychological and spiritual consequences. The first step to overcoming it is acknowledging the need for change and then embracing God's love.

Recognizing the Need for Change

The crucial initial step is to acknowledge that self-criticism is not beneficial to our spiritual or mental health. This is a difficult realization to come to, as it is easy to mistake self-criticism as a form of accountability. However, it's essential to understand that there is a clear line between constructive self-evaluation and damaging self-criticism.

The Apostle Paul, in Romans 7:15, ESV, expresses this struggle aptly: "For I do not understand my own actions. For I do not do what I want, but I do the very thing I hate." We need to comprehend that self-criticism is not helping us grow or achieve our goals but rather hindering us.

Once we acknowledge the need for change, the door is open for transformation. Acknowledgment doesn't equate to immediate change, but it's the prerequisite that allows the process of change to commence.

Embracing God's Unconditional Love

Embracing God's unconditional love is the crucial next step after acknowledging the need for change. This is the heart of the gospel message, as stated in Romans 5:8, ESV: "But God shows his love for us in that while we were still sinners, Christ died for us." God's love is not conditional on our performance or our self-worth. It is steadfast, unchanging, and offered freely to all.

As we internalize this truth, we can begin to let go of our damaging self-criticisms and replace them with God's affirmations. It's not an easy transition, and it doesn't happen overnight, but each step brings us closer to experiencing the fullness of God's love.

We can find solace in 2 Corinthians 12:9, ESV, where Paul shares God's words to him: "But he said to me, 'My grace is sufficient for you, for my power is made perfect in weakness.' Therefore I will boast all the more gladly of my weaknesses, so that the power of Christ may rest upon me."

Embracing God's love allows us to see ourselves from His perspective - as valued, loved, and worthy. It changes our internal dialogue from criticism and judgment to love, grace, and acceptance.

The Power of Prayer

Prayer is a powerful tool in this process. It's not only a way to communicate with God, but it's also a way to refocus our thoughts and reinforce the truth of God's love in our minds.

We can pray as David did in Psalm 139:23-24, ASV: "Search me, O God, and know my heart: Try me, and know my thoughts; And see if there be any wicked way in me, And lead me in the way everlasting."

Conclusion: Walking in Love

As we acknowledge the need for change and embrace God's love, we embark on a journey of transformation. Self-criticism gradually loses its hold, replaced by the truth of God's love. As we internalize this love, we can extend it to others, demonstrating the love of Christ in our actions and words.

This transformation isn't instantaneous; it's a journey. But it's a journey worth embarking on, one that leads to improved mental health, deeper spiritual understanding, and a more fulfilling relationship with God and those around us.

As we walk this path, we are reminded of Romans 8:1, ESV, "There is therefore now no condemnation for those who are in Christ Jesus." When we live in the light of this truth, we're not just overcoming self-criticism. We are embracing our identity as children of God, loved unconditionally and called to a purpose-filled life.

Discovering God's Unconditional Love

Exploring the Depth of God's Love and Grace for Us

After acknowledging the need for change and beginning to embrace God's love, we are poised to explore the depth of God's love and grace for us. This exploration is essential because it forms the basis for our understanding of self and our interactions with others. The more we grasp the extent of God's love and grace, the more we can reflect these attributes in our own lives.

God's Love: Infinite and Unchanging

The love of God is a theme that courses through the entire Bible. It's an immense love that remains steadfast and constant, unaffected by our actions or inactions. In Jeremiah 31:3, ASV, God says to His people, "Yea, I have loved thee with an everlasting love: therefore with lovingkindness have I drawn thee."

God's love is not merely an emotional feeling; it's a commitment, a promise, a covenant. It doesn't fluctuate with our performance or our self-perceptions. This love is so profound that Paul, in Romans 8:38-39, ESV, wrote, "For I am sure that neither death nor life, nor angels nor rulers, nor things present nor things to come, nor powers, nor height nor depth, nor anything else in all creation, will be able to separate us from the love of God in Christ Jesus our Lord." The depth of God's love is such that nothing can separate us from it.

God's Grace: A Gift Unearned

Grace is another component of God's relationship with us that's difficult to fully comprehend. By its very definition, grace is unmerited favor - it's receiving good things that we don't deserve and haven't earned.

The Apostle Paul says in Ephesians 2:8-9, ESV, "For by grace you have been saved through faith. And this is not your own doing; it is the gift of God, not a result of works, so that no one may boast." Grace is God's gift, freely given to us, not something we can earn or attain by our efforts. It's an extension of His infinite love for us.

Experiencing God's Love and Grace

While understanding God's love and grace intellectually is crucial, experiencing them is transformational. In Ephesians 3:18-19, ESV, Paul prays that the Ephesians "may have strength to comprehend with all the saints what is the breadth and length and height and depth, and to know the love of Christ that surpasses knowledge, that you may be filled with all the fullness of God."

To experience God's love and grace, we need to invite them into our hearts, allowing them to replace the self-criticism and negative self-perceptions that have taken root. We need to remind ourselves daily of God's love and grace, reading the Scriptures, praying, and connecting with fellow believers who can encourage us and reflect God's love to us.

Conclusion: A Love Beyond Measure

As we explore the depth of God's love and grace, we discover a love beyond measure, a grace beyond comprehension. This love and grace transform us, not only changing our self-perception but also empowering us to extend this same love and grace to others.

In 1 John 4:19, ESV, we find a simple, yet profound truth: "We love because he first loved us." As we deeply understand and embrace God's love, we learn to love ourselves and others better, creating a ripple effect that extends beyond us and into the world around us. It's a powerful testament to the difference one can make when grounded in God's love and grace.

Examining Biblical Passages that Highlight God's Unfailing Love

Now that we've begun to delve into the depth of God's love and grace, it is crucial to explore further the scriptural passages that underline His unfailing love. This exploration is not a mere academic exercise. Instead, it's about letting God's Word permeate our hearts and minds, displacing self-criticism with His infinite love.

God's Love in the Old Testament

God's love is evident right from the beginning of the Bible, in the book of Genesis. When Adam and Eve sinned in the Garden of Eden, God could have abandoned them. But instead, He provided a covering for them (Genesis 3:21, ASV), a symbolic act of His protective love.

In Exodus 34:6-7, ASV, God describes Himself to Moses, saying, "The Lord, The Lord, a God merciful and gracious, slow to anger, and abundant in lovingkindness and truth; keeping lovingkindness for thousands, forgiving iniquity and transgression and sin." Here, we see God's loving nature explicitly spelled out.

Isaiah 54:10, ASV, offers another profound image of God's love: "For the mountains may depart, and the hills be removed; but my lovingkindness shall not depart from thee, neither shall my covenant of peace be removed, saith Jehovah that hath mercy on thee." God's love is more enduring than even the most steadfast parts of creation.

God's Love in the New Testament

In the New Testament, God's love is not only reiterated but also embodied in the person and work of Jesus Christ. In John 3:16, ESV, one of the most famous verses in the Bible, we read, "For God so loved the world, that he gave his only Son, that whoever believes in him should not perish but have eternal life." God's love was so deep that He gave what was most precious to Him.

Romans 5:8, ESV, further demonstrates God's love in action: "But God shows his love for us in that while we were still sinners, Christ died for us." His love isn't dependent on our goodness or worthiness. It's an initiating, pursuing love.

In 1 John 4:9-10, ESV, we read, "In this the love of God was made manifest among us, that God sent his only Son into the world, so that we might live through him. In this is love, not that we have loved God but that he loved us and sent his Son to be the propitiation for our sins."

Conclusion: A Love Letter Written in Blood

The entire Bible, from Genesis to Revelation, is a testament to God's unfailing love for us. As we explore these and other passages, we discover that His Word isn't a dry textbook or a list of rules, but a love letter written in blood on the cross of Calvary.

The scriptures remind us that, despite our self-criticisms and perceived inadequacies, we are deeply loved by the Creator of the universe. This love doesn't just forgive our sins; it also affirms our worth, heals our wounds, and equips us to love ourselves and others in the same way.

The depth of God's love is a well we'll never exhaust. The more we delve into it, the more we'll find. The more we immerse ourselves in it, the more it will transform us. And the more we share it with others, the more we'll see that we indeed can make a difference, because His love has made a difference in us.

Challenging Negative Thought Patterns

Identifying and Challenging Self-Critical Thoughts and Beliefs

Self-criticism is a habit that can creep up on us subtly. It can begin innocently, perhaps with a desire to improve or meet certain expectations. However, over time, it can evolve into a constant internal dialogue of negative self-judgment. This can impact our mental health and impede our capacity to experience the depth of God's love. As Christians, we need to identify and challenge these self-critical thoughts and beliefs, replacing them with the truths of God's word.

Identifying Self-Critical Thoughts

First, we must recognize that self-critical thoughts often operate like background noise. We might be so accustomed to the soundtrack of self-doubt that we don't realize it's playing. So, the first step is to consciously pay attention to your thoughts.

Watch out for thoughts that involve absolute terms like "always" and "never" or those that tend to generalize from a single event. For example, a single mistake at work might prompt thoughts like, "I always mess things up" or "I'm never good at this job." These are warning signs of a self-critical mindset.

Challenging Self-Critical Thoughts with Scripture

Once we've identified self-critical thoughts, we can counter them with the truth of Scripture. The Bible doesn't just tell us about God's love; it also tells us about our value in His eyes.

For instance, when we think, "I'm worthless," we can counter this with Psalm 139:14, ASV, which says, "I will give thanks unto thee; for I am fearfully and wonderfully made: Wonderful are thy works; And that my soul knoweth right well."

When we think, "I'm not enough," we can remember 2 Corinthians 12:9, ESV, where God tells Paul, "My grace is sufficient for you, for my power is made perfect in weakness."

When we think, "I'm unlovable," we should remember Romans 8:38-39, ESV, which says, "For I am sure that neither death nor life, nor angels nor rulers, nor things present nor things to come, nor powers, nor height nor depth, nor anything else in all creation, will be able to separate us from the love of God in Christ Jesus our Lord."

Harnessing the Power of Prayer and Meditation

Prayer and meditation can also be powerful tools in overcoming self-criticism. We can bring our self-critical thoughts to God in prayer, asking Him to replace these lies with His truth. As we meditate on Scripture, we let its truths saturate our minds, reshaping our thinking patterns.

Philippians 4:8, ESV, provides a framework for healthy thought: "Finally, brothers, whatever is true, whatever is honorable, whatever is just, whatever is pure, whatever is lovely, whatever is commendable, if there is any excellence, if there is anything worthy of praise, think about these things."

Conclusion: The Journey Towards Self-Compassion

Overcoming self-criticism is a journey, and it can be a challenging one. But we can rest assured that as we make the effort to identify and challenge self-critical thoughts, God will be with us every step of the way, renewing our minds and transforming us into His image. As we replace self-criticism with self-compassion and acceptance, we'll be better equipped to extend that same love and compassion to others, making a difference in the world around us.

Learning to Replace Self-Critical Thoughts with God's Truth and Positive Affirmations

Once we've identified and challenged self-critical thoughts, the next step is to replace them with God's truth and positive affirmations. This process isn't about manufacturing false positivity or ignoring reality. Instead, it's about consciously choosing to focus on God's promises and aligning our thoughts with His perspective.

Understanding the Power of God's Truth

God's truth isn't just a collection of abstract theological concepts. It's a living, powerful reality that can transform our lives. Hebrews 4:12, ESV, says, "For the word of God is living and active, sharper than any two-edged sword, piercing to the division of soul and of spirit, of joints and of marrow, and discerning the thoughts and intentions of the heart." When we intentionally replace self-critical thoughts with the truth of God's word, we invite His life-giving power into our hearts and minds.

Practicing Positive Affirmations Rooted in Scripture

Positive affirmations can be a helpful tool in this process, but as Christians, our affirmations should be rooted in Scripture, reflecting the truth of who God is and who we are in Him.

Consider these examples:

- When self-criticism says, "I'm not enough," we can affirm, "I am complete in Christ," referencing Colossians 2:10, ESV: "And you have been filled in him, who is the head of all rule and authority."
- When self-criticism says, "I'm unlovable," we can affirm, "I am dearly loved by God," reminding ourselves of Jeremiah 31:3, ASV: "Jehovah appeared of old unto me, saying, Yea, I have loved thee with an everlasting love: therefore with lovingkindness have I drawn thee."
- When self-criticism says, "I'm a failure," we can affirm, "I am more than a conqueror through Christ," remembering Romans 8:37, ESV: "No, in all these things we are more than conquerors through him who loved us."

The Role of Prayer and Meditation

Prayer and meditation play crucial roles in this process. We should pray for God to renew our minds and help us to see ourselves as He sees us. "Do not be conformed to this world, but be transformed by the renewal of your mind," says Romans 12:2, ESV. As we meditate on God's word, we allow its truth to replace the lies of self-criticism.

Creating a Habit of Positive Thinking

Replacing self-critical thoughts with God's truth isn't a one-time act; it's a lifelong practice. We need to cultivate a habit of positive thinking rooted in the truths of God's word. This takes time and intentionality, but the benefits are immense.

Conclusion: The Transformative Power of God's Love

As we consistently replace self-critical thoughts with the truth of God's love and positive affirmations rooted in Scripture, we will experience a transformation. Our self-image will begin to align more closely with God's image of us. Self-criticism will give way to self-acceptance, and we will be better positioned to accept God's unconditional love and share that love with others.

Remember, the goal isn't to become self-focused but to become so grounded in God's love and truth that self-criticism no longer has a place to reside. As we grow in this, we will be equipped to make a meaningful difference in the lives of others, living out our Christian life to its fullest potential.

Embracing Forgiveness and Redemption

Accepting God's Forgiveness and Forgiving Ourselves for Past Mistakes

One of the major sources of self-criticism and self-condemnation is the burden of past mistakes. It's human nature to regret, to dwell on our failures, and to beat ourselves up over the things we wish we had done differently. However, this is not the life God intends for us. He offers us a path to freedom from this burden—through accepting His forgiveness and extending that forgiveness to ourselves.

The Profound Reality of God's Forgiveness

The Bible is clear on God's stance towards our sins when we confess and repent—He forgives us completely. As 1 John 1:9, ESV, affirms, "If we confess our sins, he is faithful and just to forgive us our sins and to cleanse us from all unrighteousness." This verse underscores two key attributes of God: His faithfulness and His justice.

God's faithfulness means that He always does what He promises. His justice means that He cannot overlook sin, but through the sacrifice of Jesus Christ on the cross, our sins have been paid for in full. This allows God to forgive us without compromising His justice.

The Psalmist beautifully captures God's forgiveness in Psalm 103:12, ASV: "As far as the east is from the west, so far hath he removed our transgressions from us." This verse uses a powerful image to express the profound reality of God's forgiveness. When God forgives us, our sins are not just swept under the rug. They are utterly removed from us, as far as the east is from the west—a distance that is essentially immeasurable.

The Challenge of Forgiving Ourselves

Yet, while we may intellectually understand and even heartily believe in God's forgiveness, forgiving ourselves can be a much greater challenge. Self-condemnation can be a relentless voice in our heads, constantly reminding us of our past failures. However, holding onto past mistakes is not a sign of humility, as some may believe. Rather, it disrespects the very heart of the Gospel message and the work that Christ accomplished on the cross.

Romans 8:1, ESV, proclaims a liberating truth: "There is therefore now no condemnation for those who are in Christ Jesus." If we are in Christ, God does not condemn us. So, if God does not condemn us, who are we to condemn ourselves?

Steps Towards Self-Forgiveness

Forgiving ourselves requires acknowledging our failures, accepting God's forgiveness, and making a conscious decision to not allow our past mistakes to dictate our self-worth or future actions.

A practical way to do this is by writing down our mistakes, confessing them to God, and consciously accepting His forgiveness. Next, we write down God's promises of forgiveness from the Scriptures. Every time self-condemnatory thoughts arise, we counter them with God's promises.

Conclusion: The Freedom in Forgiveness

As we learn to accept God's forgiveness and forgive ourselves, we begin to experience a new level of freedom and peace. Self-criticism gives way to self-acceptance, and we become better equipped to extend grace and forgiveness to others.

By letting go of past mistakes, we make room for God's love to fill us more completely, transforming us from the inside out. This inner transformation then impacts how we live our lives, enabling us to make a significant difference in the world around us—truly embodying the truth that we, as Christians, can indeed make a difference.

Embracing the Redemptive Power of God's Love to Transform Our Lives

Understanding God's love is one thing, but allowing it to permeate and transform our lives is another. Many of us struggle with self-criticism and negative self-perception because we fail to fully grasp and embrace the redemptive power of God's love. This love is not a generic, distant sentiment, but a tangible, transformative force that can radically change our lives.

God's Love: A Transformative Power

God's love is not just a feeling or a concept—it is a powerful, life-altering force that changes us from the inside out. The Apostle Paul beautifully captures this truth in 2 Corinthians 5:17, ESV: "Therefore, if anyone is in Christ, he is a new creation. The old has passed away; behold, the new has come." This verse affirms that when we come to Christ, we are not just improved, adjusted, or reformed—we are utterly and completely made new.

Experiencing Redemption through God's Love

The redemptive power of God's love can free us from the shackles of self-criticism and lead us to a place of profound self-acceptance. This is not about being complacent with our imperfections, but about understanding that God's love for us is not contingent on our performance, achievements, or the absence of mistakes in our lives.

Ephesians 2:4-5, ESV, reads: "But God, being rich in mercy, because of the great love with which he loved us, even when we were dead in our trespasses, made us alive together with Christ—by grace you have been saved." This passage affirms that even in our lowest state, God's love sought us out and breathed life into us. The redemptive power of His love is not based on our worthiness but His grace.

Letting God's Love Shape Us

We need to be active participants in this transformation process, not passive observers. This involves several steps:

1. **Acknowledge Our Worth in God's Eyes**: Psalm 139:13-14, ASV, asserts that we are wonderfully made. Embracing this truth helps us combat self-critical thoughts and perceptions.
2. **Reflect on God's Word**: Regularly reading and meditating on the Scriptures helps us understand God's love more deeply and allows His truths to replace our negative self-perceptions.
3. **Let God's Love Influence Our Thoughts and Actions**: God's love is not just meant to be experienced—it's meant to transform us. This includes the way we think about ourselves and others, and the way we live our lives.

God's Love: The Pathway to Transformation

When we truly embrace the redemptive power of God's love, we open the door to a life of transformation. Instead of being trapped in self-criticism, we begin to see ourselves as God sees us: beloved, valuable, and capable of making a difference in the world.

By allowing God's love to fill and overflow us, we become channels of His love to others, impacting their lives and showing them a glimpse of God's heart. In doing so, we embody the message that as Christians, we can indeed make a significant difference, not just in our lives, but in the lives of those around us.

Cultivating Self-Compassion

Learning to Extend Grace and Compassion to Ourselves

One of the most critical and yet often overlooked aspects of overcoming self-criticism is learning to extend grace and compassion to ourselves. Much like God's grace towards us, we need to learn to offer ourselves the same understanding, forgiveness, and gentleness we would extend to others.

God's Grace: The Model of Compassion

Understanding God's grace towards us is the foundation for learning to extend compassion to ourselves. Ephesians 2:8-9, ESV, states, "For by grace you have been saved through faith. And this is not your own doing; it is the gift of God, not a result of works, so that no one may boast." This profound statement of faith reminds us that God's love and mercy are gifts freely given, not earned. If God, who is perfect, can extend such grace to us, who are imperfect, should we not also extend such grace to ourselves?

Identifying and Challenging Self-Critical Thoughts

The first step in learning to extend grace and compassion to ourselves is to identify and challenge our self-critical thoughts. These are the inner voices that tell us we're not good enough, we're failures, or we'll never amount to anything. They are distortions of reality, not reflections of truth.

As we learn to identify these self-critical thoughts, we can begin to counter them with the truth of God's Word. Romans 8:1, ESV, assures us, "There is therefore now no condemnation for those who are in Christ Jesus." This means that no matter what our self-critical thoughts say, God does not condemn us.

Practicing Self-Compassion

Once we've begun to challenge our self-critical thoughts, we can begin practicing self-compassion. This involves treating ourselves with kindness and understanding when we fail or make mistakes, rather than harshly criticizing ourselves.

Colossians 3:12, ESV, exhorts us to "Put on then, as God's chosen ones, holy and beloved, compassionate hearts, kindness, humility, meekness, and patience." As we grow in our understanding of God's grace, we can apply these qualities to ourselves, extending grace and compassion to ourselves when we fall short.

Reaping the Benefits of Self-Compassion

By extending grace and compassion to ourselves, we align ourselves more closely with God's heart. We learn to see ourselves as God sees us: flawed, yes, but also deeply loved and capable of growth and transformation. This can lead to increased self-esteem, greater mental and emotional health, and a deeper relationship with God.

Conclusion

God's grace offers a model of compassion that we can extend to ourselves. By identifying and challenging our self-critical thoughts and practicing self-compassion, we can move beyond self-criticism and live in the freedom and peace that God offers. This is not an overnight process, but a journey of ongoing growth and transformation, powered by God's unending love for us.

Embracing Our Inherent Worth as Children of God

One of the most empowering and liberating truths that can overcome self-criticism is the recognition of our inherent worth as children of God. This is a central tenet of the Christian faith and a deeply transformative truth that can shift the way we perceive ourselves and interact with the world.

Understanding Our Identity in Christ

The first step in embracing our inherent worth is understanding our identity in Christ. This is not based on our achievements, failures, or self-perceptions. Instead, it is rooted in God's declaration of our worth.

In John 1:12, ESV, it states, "But to all who did receive him, who believed in his name, he gave the right to become children of God." This is a profound statement of identity. Regardless of our mistakes, imperfections, or the negative self-talk we might engage in, our value in the eyes of God remains the same - we are His children.

Challenging Negative Self-Perceptions

Negative self-perceptions often stem from a flawed understanding of our identity and worth. We may mistakenly believe that our value is contingent upon external factors such as our success, attractiveness, or the approval of others. These false beliefs can fuel self-critical thoughts and negative self-talk.

However, the Bible offers a radically different perspective. According to Psalm 139:14, ASV, "I will give thanks unto thee; for I am fearfully and wonderfully made: Wonderful are thy works; And that my soul knoweth right well." Our worth is not dependent on transient, worldly factors. Instead, it is grounded in the unchanging truth that we are fearfully and wonderfully made by God Himself.

Affirming Our Worth in Christ

Once we have identified and challenged negative self-perceptions, the next step is to affirm our worth in Christ regularly. We can do this through prayer, meditation on Scripture, and other spiritual practices. These activities help engrain the truth of our divine worth into our minds and hearts, gradually replacing self-critical thoughts with positive, God-centered affirmations.

Romans 8:38-39, ESV, provides a powerful affirmation: "For I am sure that neither death nor life, nor angels nor rulers, nor things present nor things to come, nor powers, nor height nor depth, nor anything else in all creation, will be able to separate us from the love of God in Christ Jesus our Lord." This assurance serves as a constant reminder of our unshakeable worth in God's eyes.

Living Out Our Worth

Finally, embracing our inherent worth as children of God requires us to live out this truth in our daily lives. This means extending grace to ourselves, pursuing growth and transformation with God's help, and loving others as God loves us. The more we align our thoughts and behaviors with the reality of our divine worth, the more we can overcome self-criticism and live in the freedom and fullness that God desires for us.

Conclusion

Overcoming self-criticism involves recognizing and embracing our inherent worth as children of God. This requires understanding our identity in Christ, challenging negative self-perceptions, affirming our worth in Christ, and living out this truth in our daily lives. As we internalize and act upon this powerful reality, we can break free from the shackles of self-criticism and experience the abundant life God has for us.

Renewing the Mind with God's Word

Harnessing the Power of Scripture to Counter Self-Criticism

One of the most powerful tools at a Christian's disposal when dealing with self-criticism is the Word of God, the Bible. Scriptures, inspired and inerrant, hold the power to dispel doubts, counteract negative thoughts, and instill a firm identity in Christ.

The Power of the Word of God

Hebrews 4:12 (ESV) says, "For the word of God is living and active, sharper than any two-edged sword, piercing to the division of soul and of spirit, of joints and of marrow, and discerning the thoughts and intentions of the heart." Scriptures are not just words on a page; they are God-breathed, living, and dynamic. They have the power to expose our deepest thoughts and feelings, including those of self-doubt and self-criticism.

Scripture as a Mirror

The Scriptures act as a mirror, reflecting not just our fallen nature, but also our true identity as children of God. James 1:23-25 (ESV) uses the metaphor of a mirror: "For if anyone is a hearer of the word and not a doer, he is like a man who looks intently at his natural face in a mirror. For he looks at himself and goes away and at once forgets what he was like. But the one who looks into the perfect law, the law of liberty, and perseveres, being no hearer who forgets but a doer who acts, he will be blessed in his doing." By regularly reading and meditating on the Scriptures, we remind ourselves of our true identity and purpose in Christ, which can counteract self-critical thoughts.

Scripture for Comfort and Encouragement

Scripture is a source of great comfort and encouragement. When we are bombarded with self-critical thoughts, we can turn to God's promises. In Romans 8:1 (ESV), we find this promise: "There is therefore now no condemnation for those who are in Christ Jesus."

This scripture can be a potent antidote to self-condemnation and criticism.

The Role of Memorization and Meditation

Memorizing and meditating on Scripture is an effective way to internalize God's truth. Psalm 119:11, ASV, says, "Thy word have I laid up in my heart, that I might not sin against thee." Memorizing scripture allows God's word to be readily available in our minds to counter negative thoughts or self-criticism.

The Transformative Power of the Word

Finally, the Word of God has a transformative power that reshapes our thoughts and perspectives. As we immerse ourselves in Scripture, the Holy Spirit works within us to renew our minds. Romans 12:2 (ESV) says, "Do not be conformed to this world, but be transformed by the renewal of your mind, that by testing you may discern what is the will of God, what is good and acceptable and perfect."

Conclusion

In the battle against self-criticism, the Word of God is an indispensable weapon. As we read, memorize, and meditate on Scripture, we can counter self-critical thoughts, discover our true identity in Christ, and experience the transformative power of God's Word. By harnessing the power of Scripture, we can overcome self-criticism and live a life marked by the freedom and fullness of God's love.

Meditating on Verses That Affirm Our Identity in Christ

A significant part of overcoming self-criticism involves acknowledging and embracing our identity in Christ. The Bible offers many verses that affirm who we are as children of God. Meditating on these passages can fortify our faith, strengthen our self-perception, and ward off damaging self-critical thoughts.

Why Meditate on Scripture?

Scripture meditation isn't about emptying our minds; it's about filling them with God's Word. It involves deep thinking, pondering, and personalizing the Word of God. In Psalm 1:2 (ASV), the psalmist describes the person who is blessed as one who "delights in the law of the LORD, and on his law he meditates day and night." As we meditate on verses affirming our identity in Christ, we allow these truths to permeate our thinking, transform our self-perception, and guide our actions.

Understanding Our Identity in Christ

Understanding our identity in Christ is foundational to overcoming self-criticism. When we know who we are in God's eyes, negative self-perception loses its grip. Here are a few powerful verses that affirm our identity in Christ:

- **Chosen and Loved by God**: Ephesians 1:4-5 (ESV) says, "Even as he chose us in him before the foundation of the world, that we should be holy and blameless before him. In love he predestined us for adoption to himself as sons through Jesus Christ, according to the purpose of his will."

- **Created for Good Works**: Ephesians 2:10 (ESV) states, "For we are his workmanship, created in Christ Jesus for good works, which God prepared beforehand, that we should walk in them."

- **Heirs with Christ**: In Romans 8:17 (ESV), Paul writes, "And if children, then heirs—heirs of God and fellow heirs with Christ, provided we suffer with him in order that we may also be glorified with him."

- **God's Beloved Children**: 1 John 3:1 (ESV) declares, "See what kind of love the Father has given to us, that we should be called children of God; and so we are."

Meditating on these Verses

Meditation involves repetition, reflection, and personal application. Take one verse at a time and read it several times. Reflect on what it says about your identity in Christ. Consider its implications for your life. Then, think about how it counteracts specific self-critical thoughts you struggle with. Finally, pray about what you've learned, asking God to deepen your understanding and make these truths a reality in your life.

The Power of Scripture Meditation

The more we meditate on who we are in Christ, the more we are shaped by these truths. We start to see ourselves as God sees us—loved, chosen, valuable, and designed for a purpose. This process will not only counter self-criticism but will also empower us to live more fully as God intended.

Conclusion

Meditating on verses that affirm our identity in Christ is a powerful practice for overcoming self-criticism. As we consistently fill our minds with God's truth, we will discover a new, uplifting narrative about ourselves—one that aligns with God's view rather than a self-critical perspective. God's Word has the power to shape our identity and transform our self-perception. Let's harness this power by meditating on verses that affirm our identity in Christ.

Walking in Freedom and Confidence

Stepping into the Freedom That Comes from Embracing God's Love

Embracing God's love carries an unimaginable power that can break the chains of self-criticism and catapult us into a realm of freedom. This freedom is not merely an escape from negative thoughts but an entrance into a full, abundant life that God promises to those who believe in Him (John 10:10, ESV). As we learn to step into this freedom, we will start to see ourselves as God does, thus overcoming the damaging effects of self-criticism.

The Captivity of Self-Criticism

Self-criticism traps us in a cycle of negativity and self-condemnation. It distorts our self-perception, making us feel inadequate and unworthy. This constant barrage of self-deprecating thoughts can shackle us, preventing us from experiencing the fullness of life that God offers. Embracing God's love is the key to breaking free from this cycle.

Understanding God's Unconditional Love

To step into the freedom that God's love brings, we need to grasp its breadth, depth, and unchanging nature. In Romans 8:38-39 (ESV), the Apostle Paul states, "For I am sure that neither death nor life, nor angels nor rulers, nor things present nor things to come, nor powers, nor height nor depth, nor anything else in all creation, will be able to separate us from the love of God in Christ Jesus our Lord." This passage underscores the permanent and unfailing nature of God's love toward us.

Embracing God's Love

To embrace God's love means accepting it as an absolute truth of our lives. Regardless of our shortcomings or the negative thoughts we may have about ourselves, God's love for us remains steadfast and unchanging. In His eyes, we are precious, loved, and valuable.

The first step toward embracing God's love is acknowledging the truth of His Word. We are His beloved children (1 John 3:1, ESV), chosen and precious in His sight (1 Peter 2:4, ESV). God demonstrated His love for us by sending His only Son to die for our sins, and nothing can separate us from this love (Romans 5:8; 8:35, ESV). This belief should not just remain head knowledge but should penetrate our hearts, influencing how we perceive ourselves.

Freedom in Embracing God's Love

Freedom that comes from embracing God's love is multifaceted. It includes:

- **Freedom from guilt and condemnation**: Romans 8:1 (ESV) reassures us, "There is therefore now no condemnation for those who are in Christ Jesus."

- **Freedom from fear**: 1 John 4:18 (ESV) states, "There is no fear in love, but perfect love casts out fear."
- **Freedom to be ourselves**: As we understand and embrace God's love, we gain the freedom to be who God has created us to be, without fear of rejection or criticism.

Walking in Freedom

Stepping into freedom means living out our identity as God's beloved children in our daily lives. It's about letting God's truth shape our self-perception and guide our actions, rather than succumbing to self-criticism. This freedom allows us to live courageously, secure in the knowledge of God's unfailing love.

Conclusion

Overcoming self-criticism is a journey of stepping into the freedom that comes from embracing God's love. As we allow the truth of God's love to saturate our hearts and minds, we find ourselves freed from the bondage of self-criticism. Embracing God's love enables us to see ourselves through His eyes—a perspective that brings healing, wholeness, and a joyful sense of liberty. Let us step into this freedom and experience the life-transforming power of God's love.

Cultivating Self-Confidence Rooted in Our Identity as Beloved Children of God

A healthy self-confidence is an essential part of a balanced Christian life, yet it should not be confused with pride or self-sufficiency. When our confidence is rooted in our identity as God's beloved children, we begin to understand our value from His perspective, not the world's. This chapter will guide you on how to cultivate this kind of self-confidence, which is firmly rooted in the knowledge of our divine heritage and unconditional acceptance by God.

Understanding Biblical Self-Confidence

Biblical self-confidence is fundamentally different from the world's understanding of the concept. Worldly self-confidence often emphasizes self-reliance and personal achievement. However, biblical self-confidence is about acknowledging our dependence on God and realizing that our true worth is not based on our abilities, appearance, or achievements, but on God's love for us and our identity in Christ.

The Foundation: Our Identity in Christ

The cornerstone of biblical self-confidence is the knowledge and acceptance of our identity as God's beloved children. According to 1 John 3:1 (ESV), "See what kind of love the Father has given to us, that we should be called children of God; and so we are." This verse assures us that God's love for us is so great that He has adopted us into His family. As His children, we share in Christ's inheritance and enjoy the favor and love of our heavenly Father.

Believing and Affirming Our Identity in Christ

Building biblical self-confidence starts with believing what God's Word says about us. Romans 8:17 (ESV) states, "and if children, then heirs—heirs of God and fellow heirs with Christ." As God's children, we have been given the same status and blessings that Jesus Christ has. We are not only saved by grace, but we are also empowered to live victoriously, not in our strength, but by the power of the Holy Spirit who lives in us.

Regularly affirming our identity in Christ is a powerful tool for cultivating biblical self-confidence. It helps us to internalize these truths, gradually transforming the way we perceive ourselves. Affirmations can be simple, such as "I am a child of God," "I am loved unconditionally," or "I am an heir with Christ."

Nurturing Confidence through Spiritual Disciplines

Spiritual disciplines like prayer, Bible study, worship, and fellowship with other believers are crucial in cultivating biblical self-confidence. As we draw near to God through these practices, we continually remind ourselves of who we are in Him. Regular interaction with God's Word allows us to absorb His truths about us, further reinforcing our identity in Christ.

The Outcome: Empowered Living

A robust biblical self-confidence has profound implications for our lives. It frees us from the need to prove ourselves to others, reducing anxiety and promoting peace of mind. It enables us to serve God and others effectively, knowing that we are doing so not to earn favor but out of the overflow of God's love in us. Most importantly, it allows us to face trials with faith and courage, confident that our heavenly Father is with us.

Conclusion

Cultivating self-confidence rooted in our identity as beloved children of God requires regular engagement with God's Word, active involvement in spiritual disciplines, and a shift in our self-perception. When we base our worth on God's unwavering love for us, we are released from the burden of self-criticism and empowered to live a fulfilling, God-honoring life.

BIBLIOGRAPHY

Alcorn, R. (2009). *If God Is Good: Faith in the Midst of Suffering and Evil.* Multnomah.

Andrews, Edward D. (2023). *MERE CHRISTIANITY REIMAGINED: Rediscovering the Faith for the 21st Century.* Christian Publishing House.

Andrews, Edward D. (2017). *GOD WILL GET YOU THROUGH THIS: Hope and Help for Your Difficult Times.* Christian Publishing House.

Andrews, Edward D. (2017). *TURN OLD HABITS INTO NEW HABITS: Why and How the Bible Makes a Difference.* Christian Publishing House.

Andrews, Edward D. (2023). *FAITHFUL MINDS: A Biblical and Cognitive Behavioral Therapy Approach to Mental Health and Wellness.* Christian Publishing House.

Andrews, Edward D. (2023). *UNSHAKABLE BELIEFS: Strategies for Strengthening and Defending Your Faith.* Christian Publishing House.

Andrews, Edward D. (2023). *EVANGELICAL THEOLOGY—GOD: Essential Christian Beliefs About God.* Christian Publishing House.

Andrews, Edward D. (2009). *CHRISTIAN APOLOGETICS: Answering the Tough Questions: Evidence and Reason in Defense of the Faith.* Christian Publishing House.

Blackaby, H. & Blackaby, R. (2002). *Experiencing God: Knowing and Doing the Will of God.* B&H Books.

Bridges, J. (2006). *The Discipline of Grace: God's Role and Our Role in the Pursuit of Holiness.* NavPress.

Chan, F. (2008). *Crazy Love: Overwhelmed by a Relentless God.* David C. Cook.

DeYoung, K. (2009). *Just Do Something: A Liberating Approach to Finding God's Will.* Moody Publishers.

Ferguson, S. (2016). *The Whole Christ: Legalism, Antinomianism, and Gospel Assurance—Why the Marrow Controversy Still Matters.* Crossway.

Geiger, E., & Peck, K. (2011). *Identity: Who You Are in Christ.* B&H Books.

Habermas, Gary R. (2022). *DEALING WITH DOUBT.* Christian Publishing House.

Horton, M. (2011). *The Gospel-Driven Life: Being Good News People in a Bad News World.* Baker Books.

Keller, T. (2013). *Walking with God through Pain and Suffering.* Penguin Books.

MacArthur, J. (2006). *Twelve Ordinary Men: How the Master Shaped His Disciples for Greatness, and What He Wants to Do with You.* Thomas Nelson.

Murray, A. (1984). *Humility: The Journey Toward Holiness.* Bethany House Publishers.

Nielson, K. L. (2011). *Bible Study: Following the Ways of the Word.* P&R Publishing.

Packer, J. I. (1973). *Knowing God.* InterVarsity Press.

Piper, J. (2003). *Desiring God: Meditations of a Christian Hedonist.* Multnomah.

Piper, J., & Grudem, W. (2006). *Recovering Biblical Manhood and Womanhood: A Response to Evangelical Feminism.* Crossway.

Sproul, R. C. (2017). *Everyone's a Theologian: An Introduction to Systematic Theology.* Reformation Trust Publishing.

Stalnaker, Cecil W. (2022). *FAITH ADRIFT CHRISTIANITY: How Can We Avoid Drifting Away from God?.* Christian Publishing House.

Tripp, P. D. (2002). *Instruments in the Redeemer's Hands: People in Need of Change Helping People in Need of Change.* P&R Publishing.

Whitney, D. S. (2014). *Spiritual Disciplines for the Christian Life*. NavPress.

Willard, D. (2002). *Renovation of the Heart: Putting on the Character of Christ*. NavPress.

www.ingramcontent.com/pod-product-compliance
Lightning Source LLC
LaVergne TN
LVHW020927090426
835512LV00020B/3249